The Wisdom of Puppies

Puppyhood as a Life Path

LAINE CUNNINGHAM

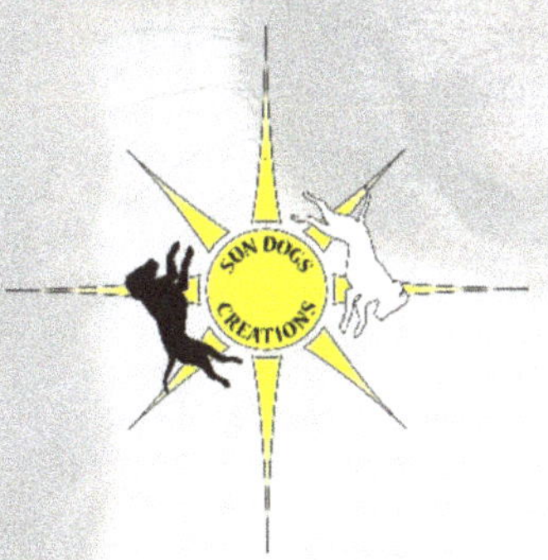

The Wisdom of Puppies
Puppyhood as a Life Path

Published by Sun Dogs Creations
Changing the World One Book at a Time
ISBN: 978-1-946732-55-2

Softcover Edition

Cover Design by Angel Leya

Introduction

Whether you're two or a hundred and two, no one can resist a puppy. From doctors to lawyers and teachers to hairdressers, a pudgy puppy pulls you away from your pressing demands and transports you to another world.

In that world, play rules. Naps are also important...very important...and a sense of adventure is required. A puppy's wide-open mind and equally open heart allow us to experience the joy and pleasure of being fully in the moment.

Sure, they lack any sense of boundaries, and they pee on our furniture for the first few weeks. But those characteristics reflect boundless curiosity and a willingness to explore. We discover that experiences are far more important than possessions.

Puppy piles, unrelenting cuteness, floppy ears and oversized paws warm the places hidden deep in our souls. Everything about puppies reminds us that the world is a big, exciting, and wonderful place. When we see through their eyes, we unearth surprises that have been under our noses the entire time.

These furry, squirmy bundles offer wisdom that is playful, joyful, and as valid for human adults as it is for young dogs. Open your mind to *The Wisdom of Puppies* and discover puppyhood as a life path.

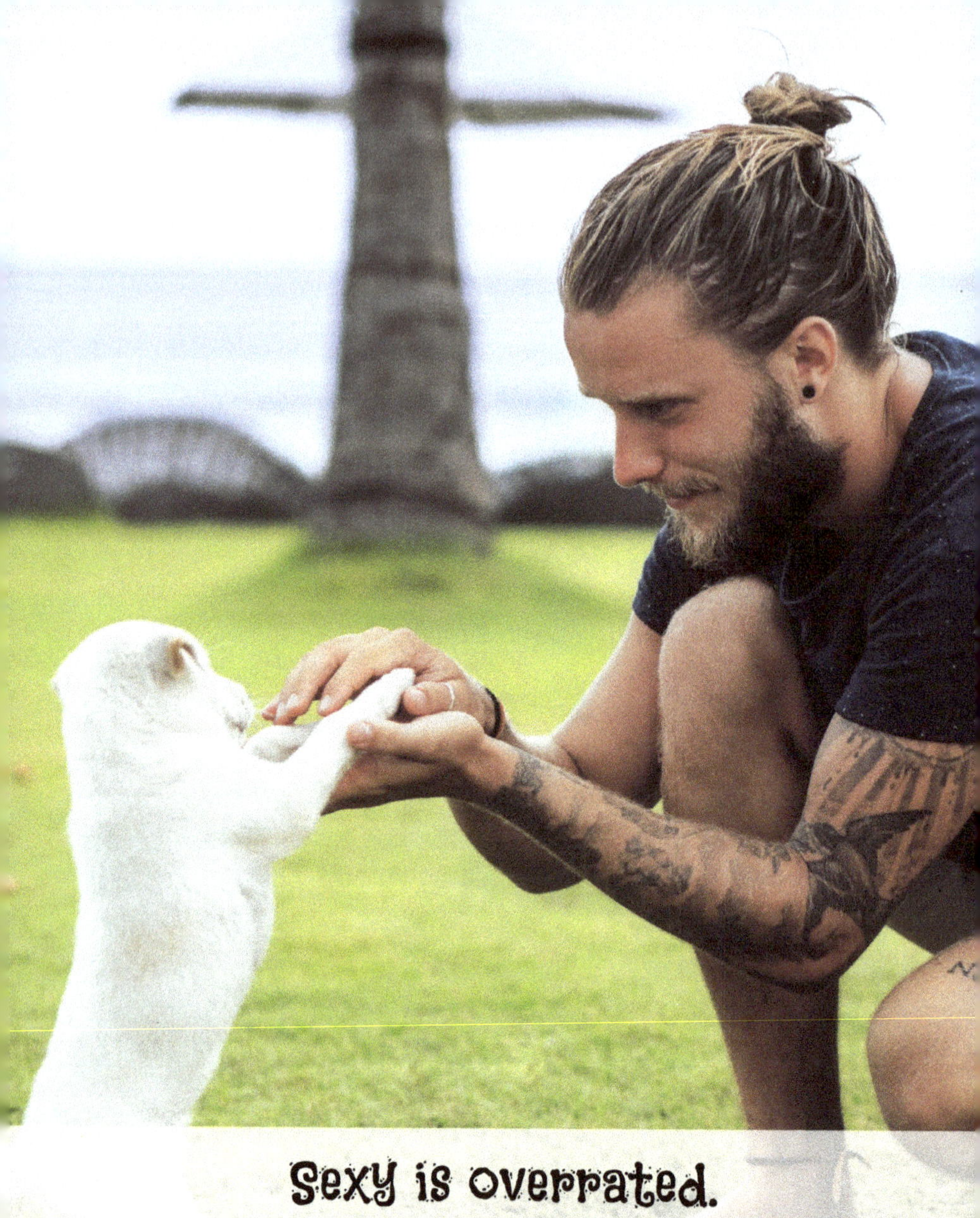

Sexy is overrated.
Cute wins every time.

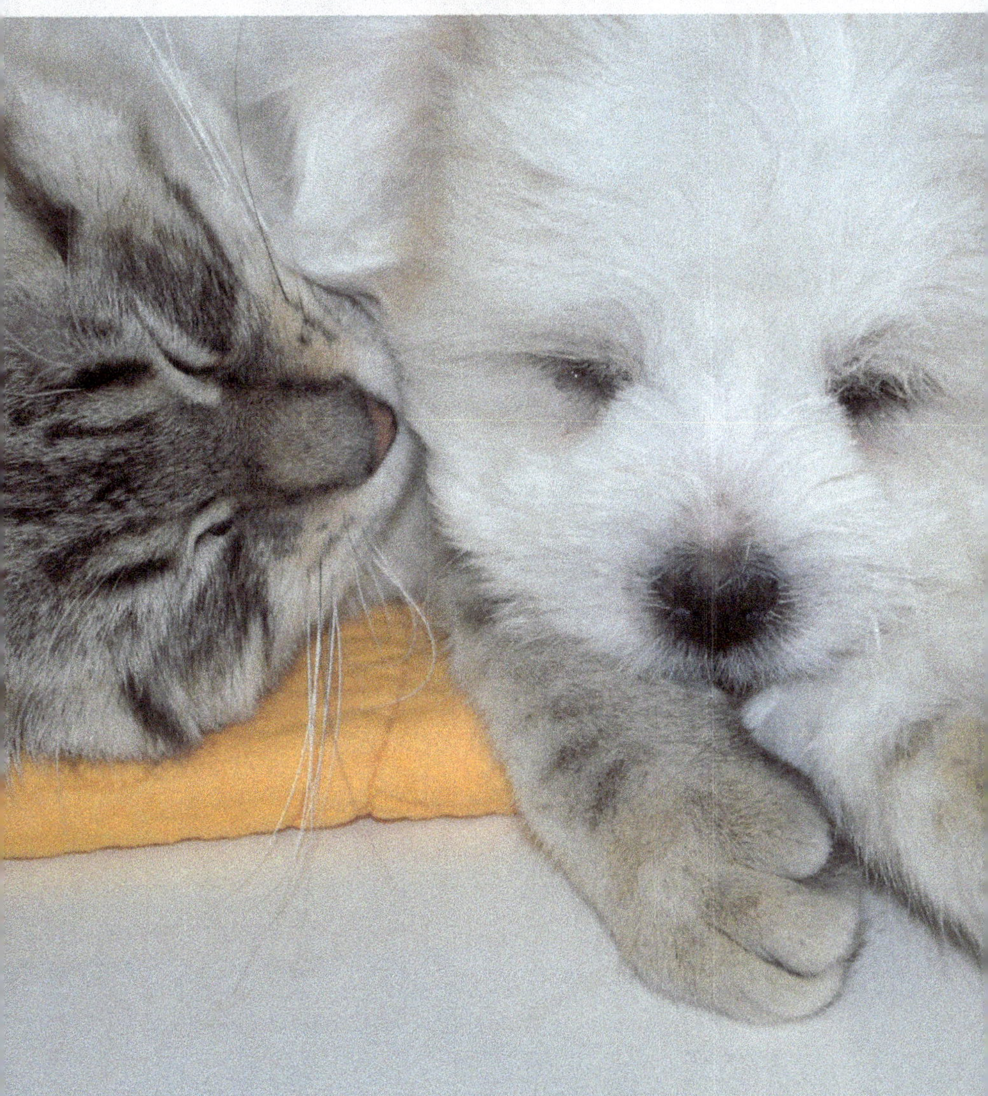

Anyone who doesn't love puppies
is probably a cat.

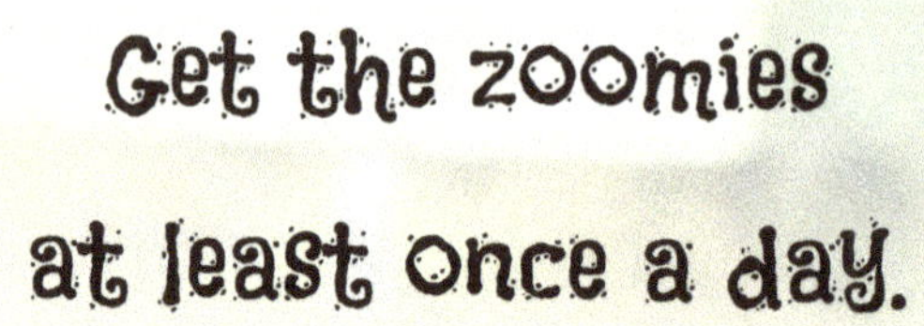

Get the zoomies
at least once a day.

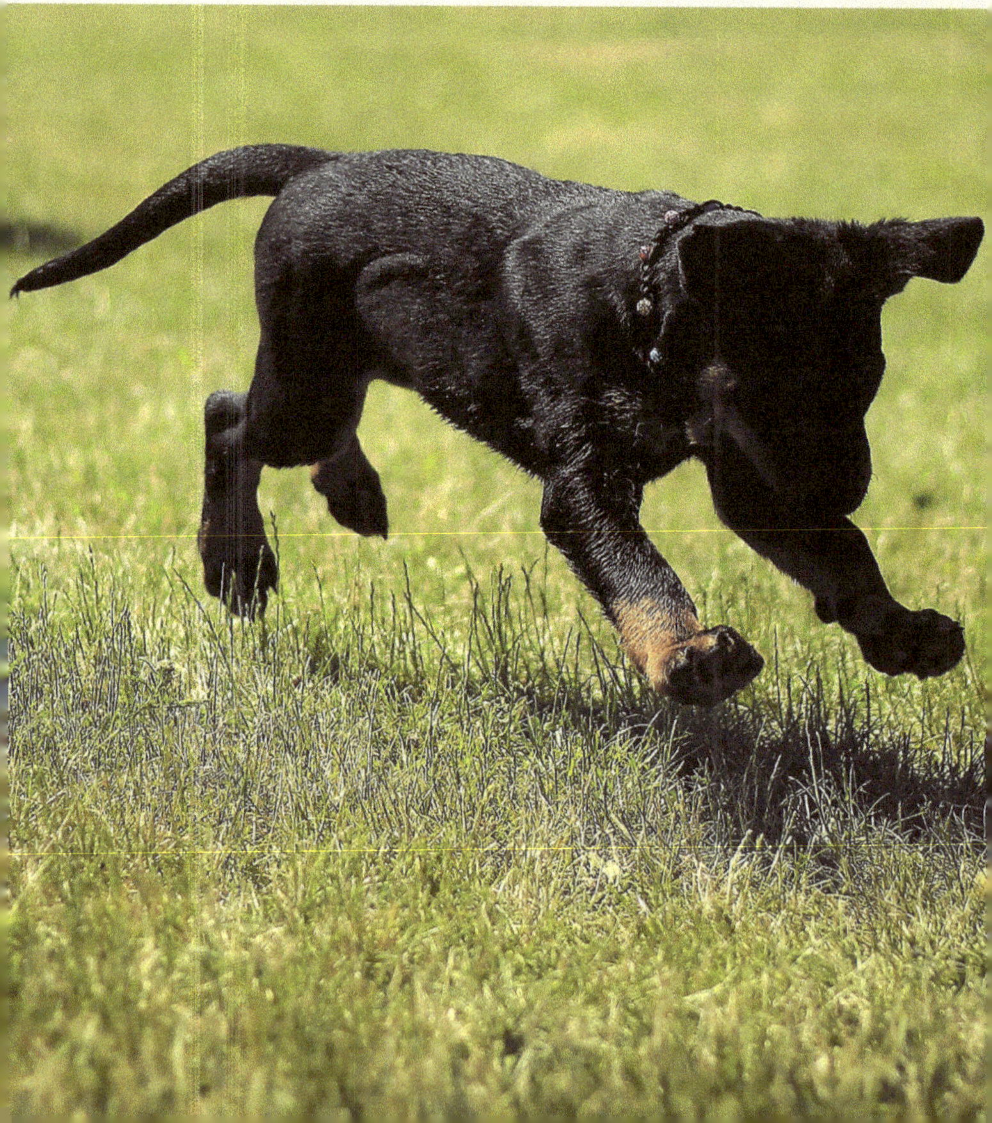

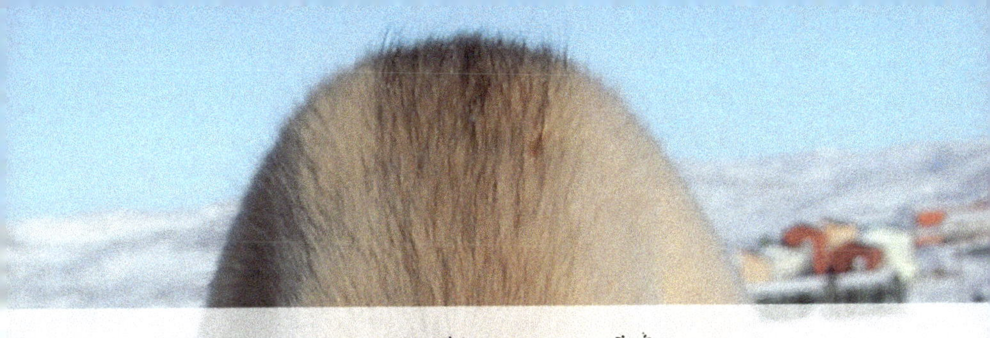

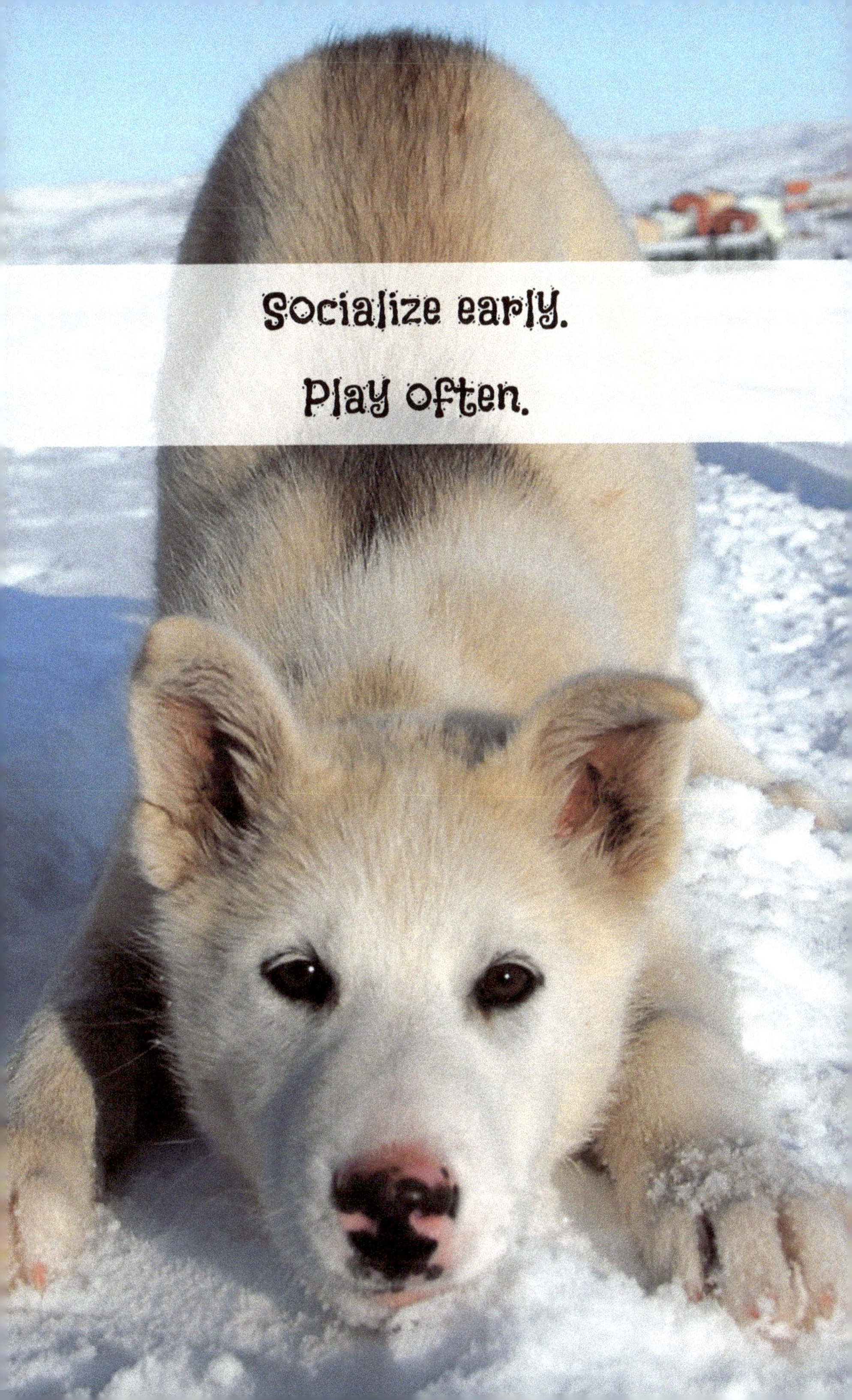

Socialize early.

Play often.

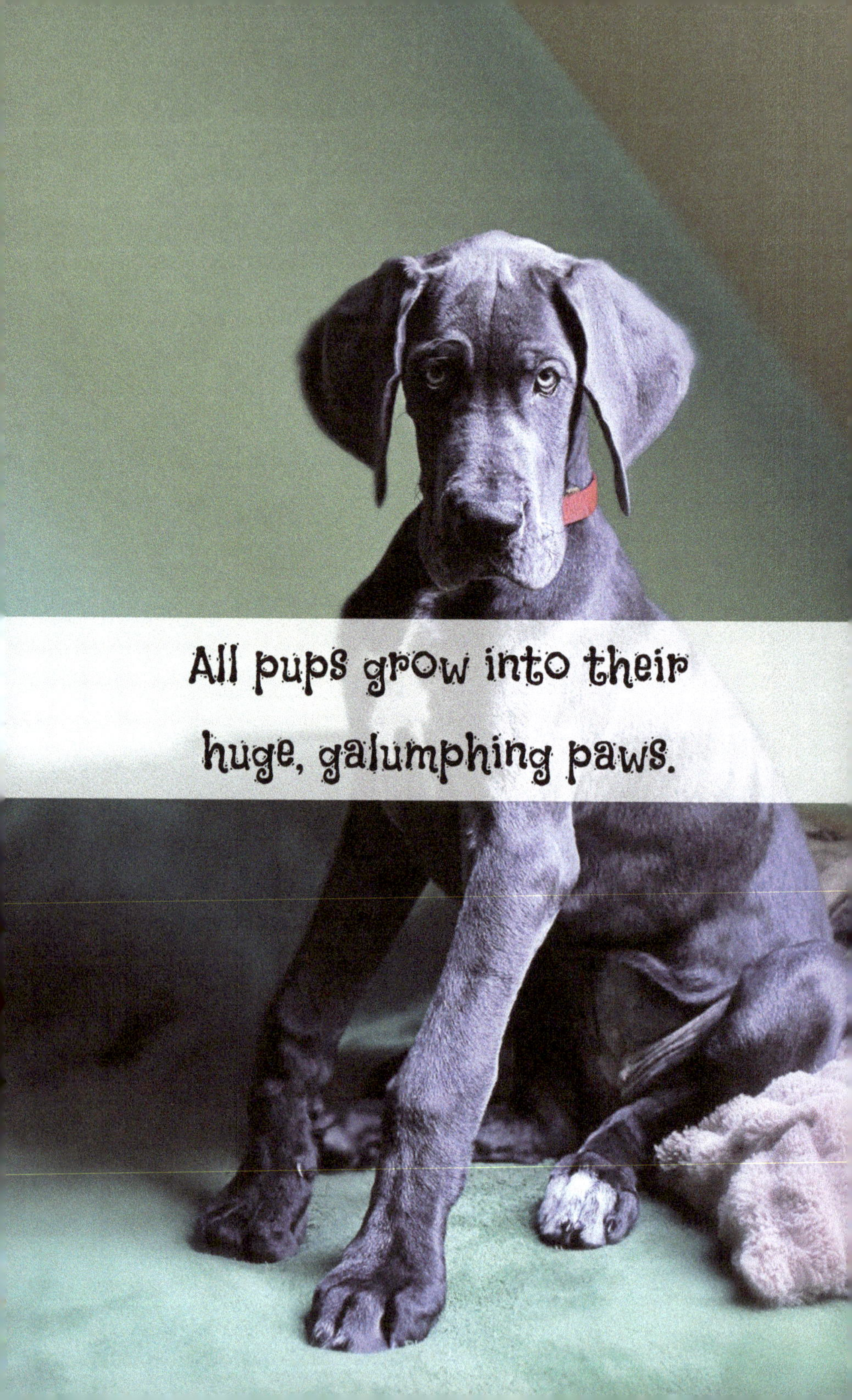

All pups grow into their

huge, galumphing paws.

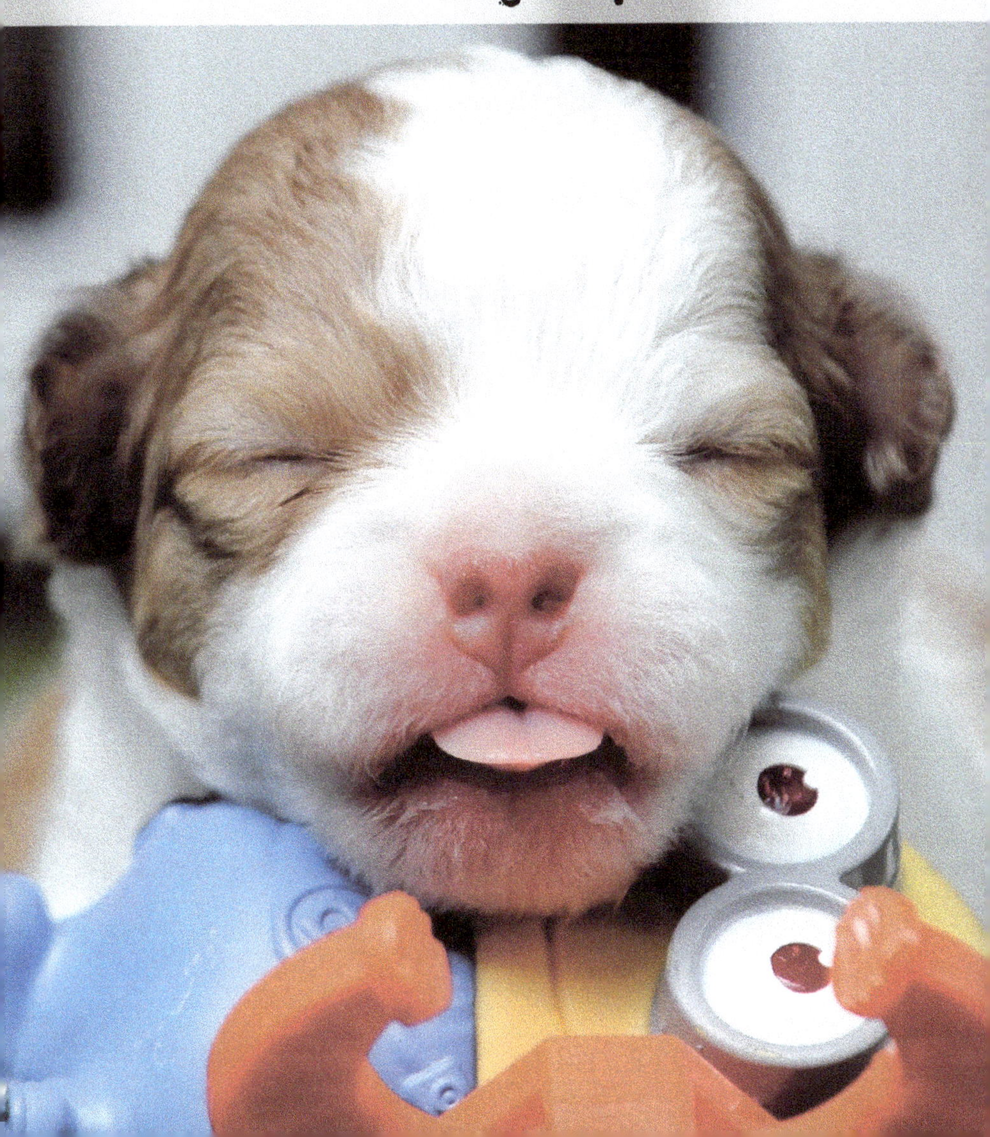

Naps can be taken
in the strangest places.

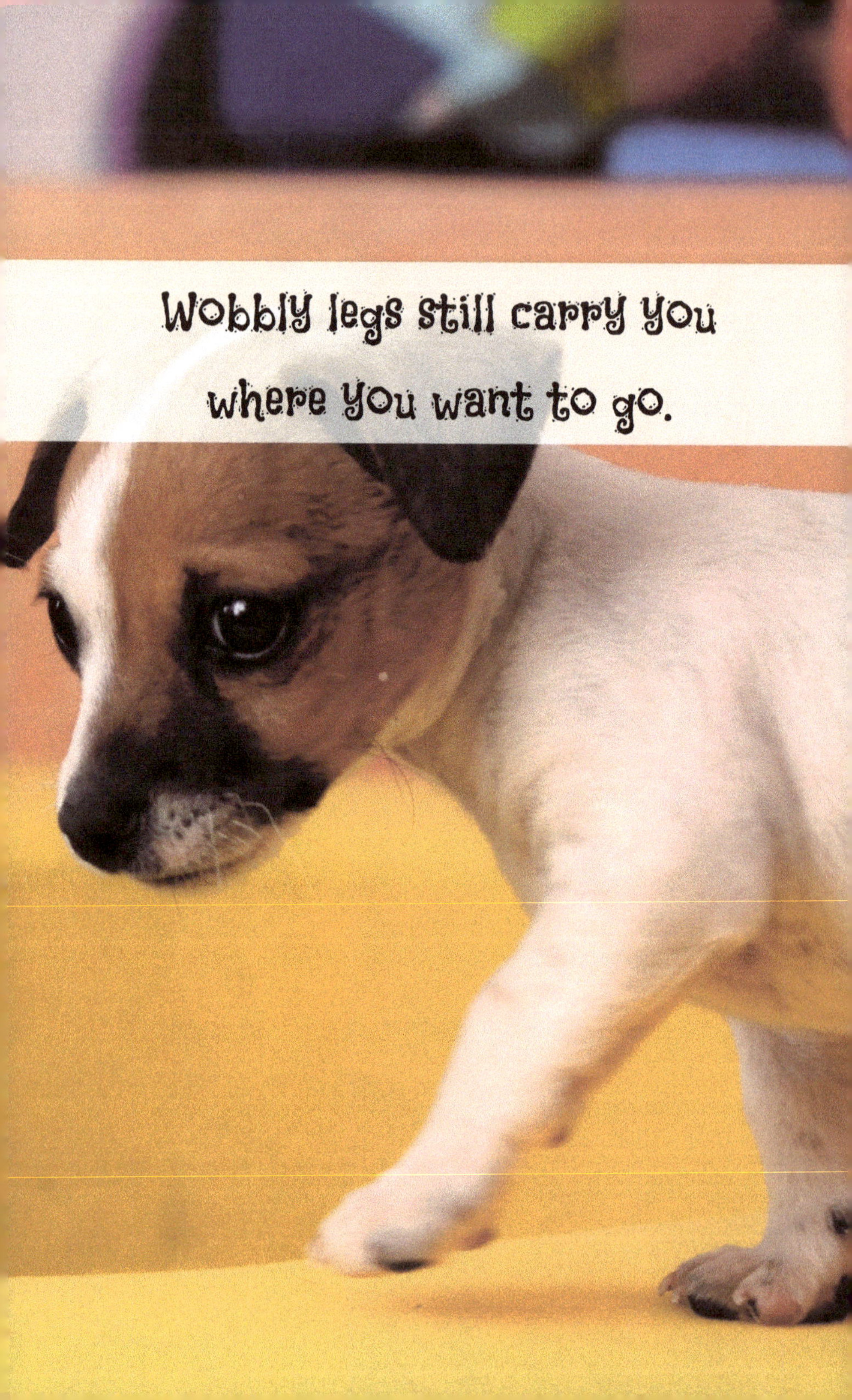

Wobbly legs still carry you
where you want to go.

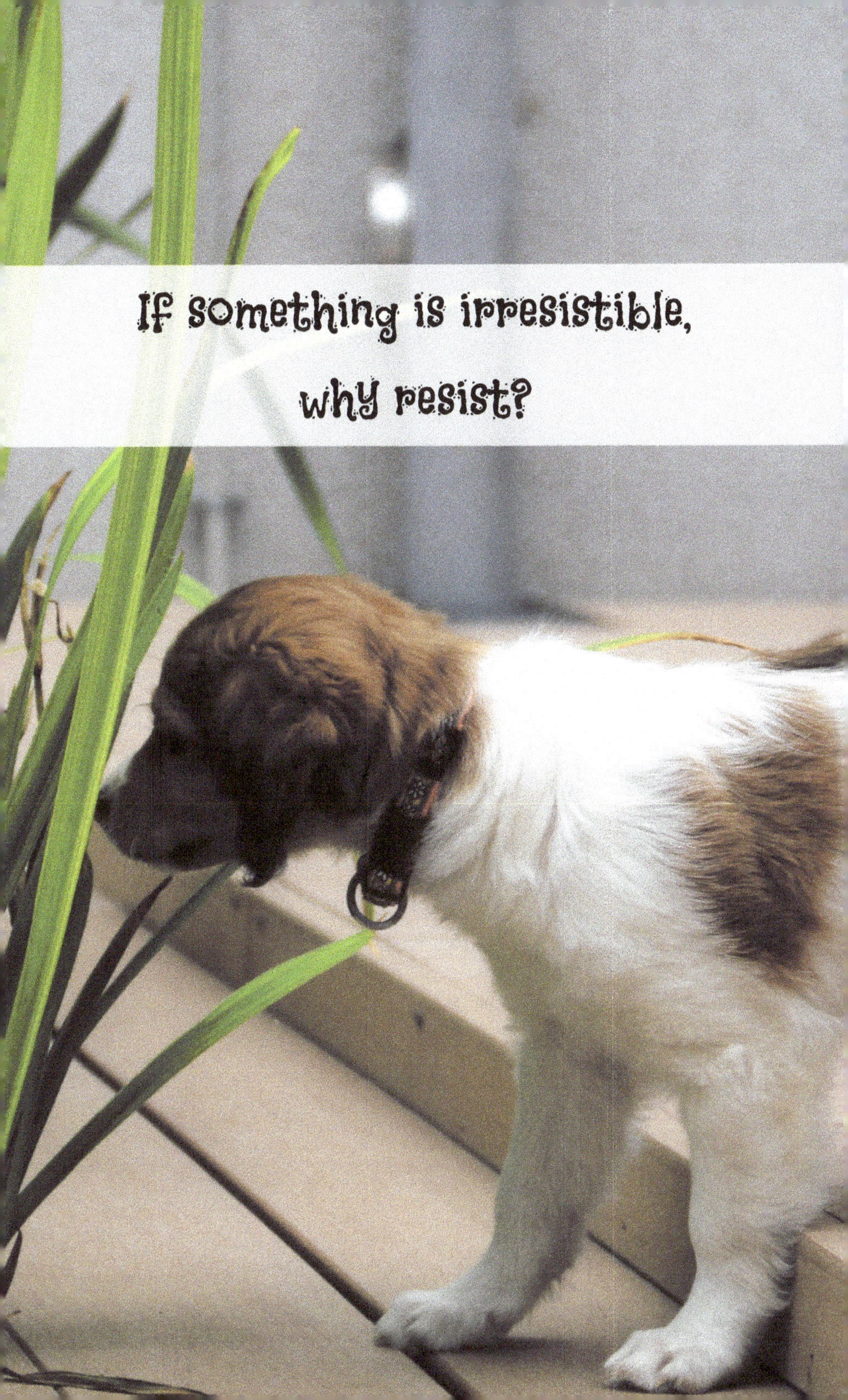

If something is irresistible,
why resist?

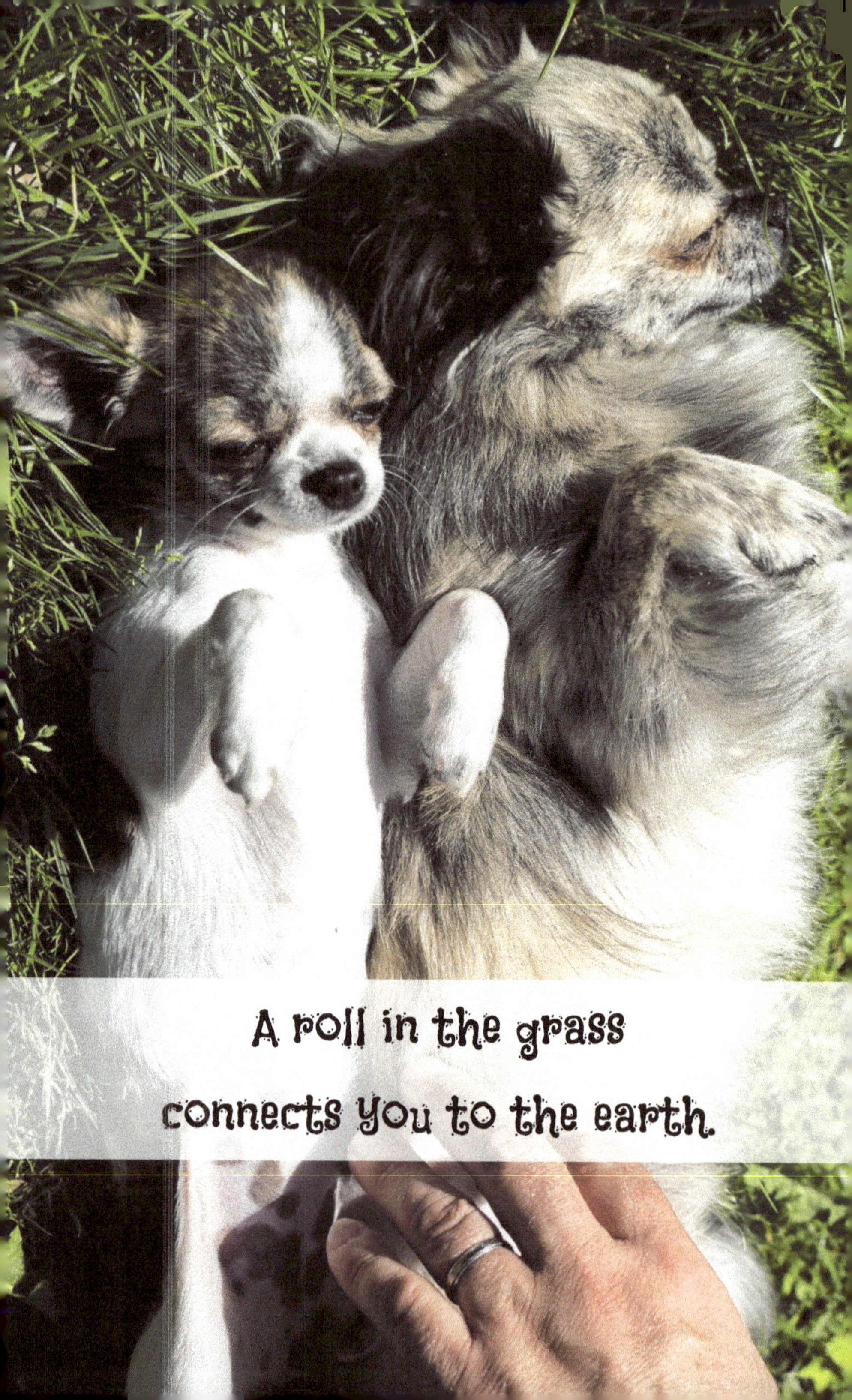

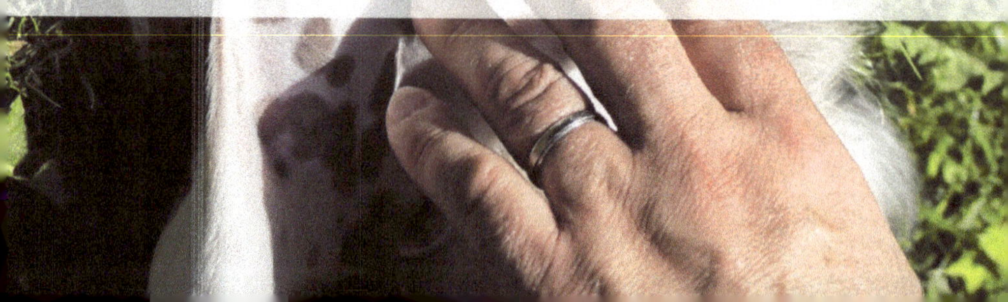
A roll in the grass
connects you to the earth.

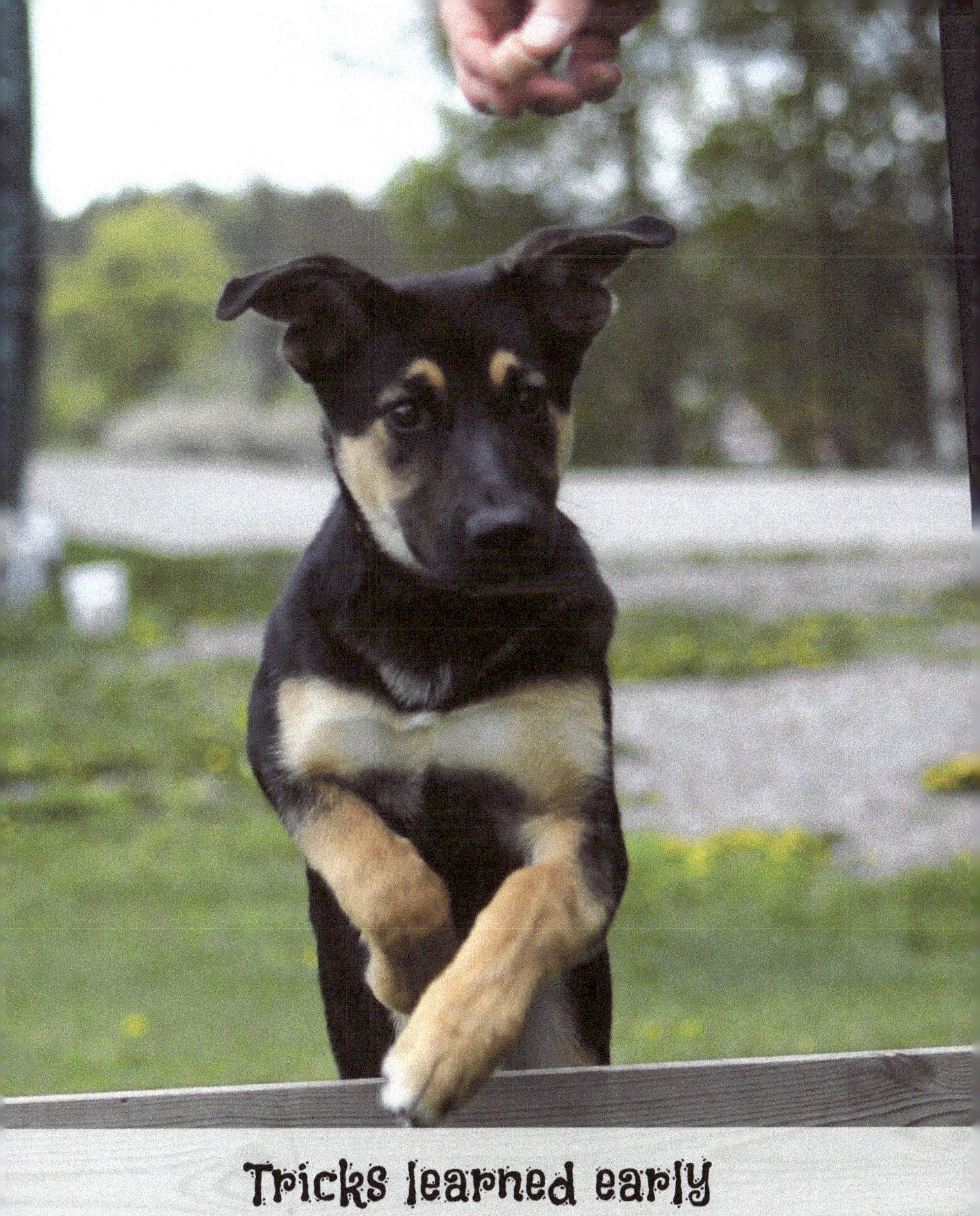
Tricks learned early
garner treats for life.

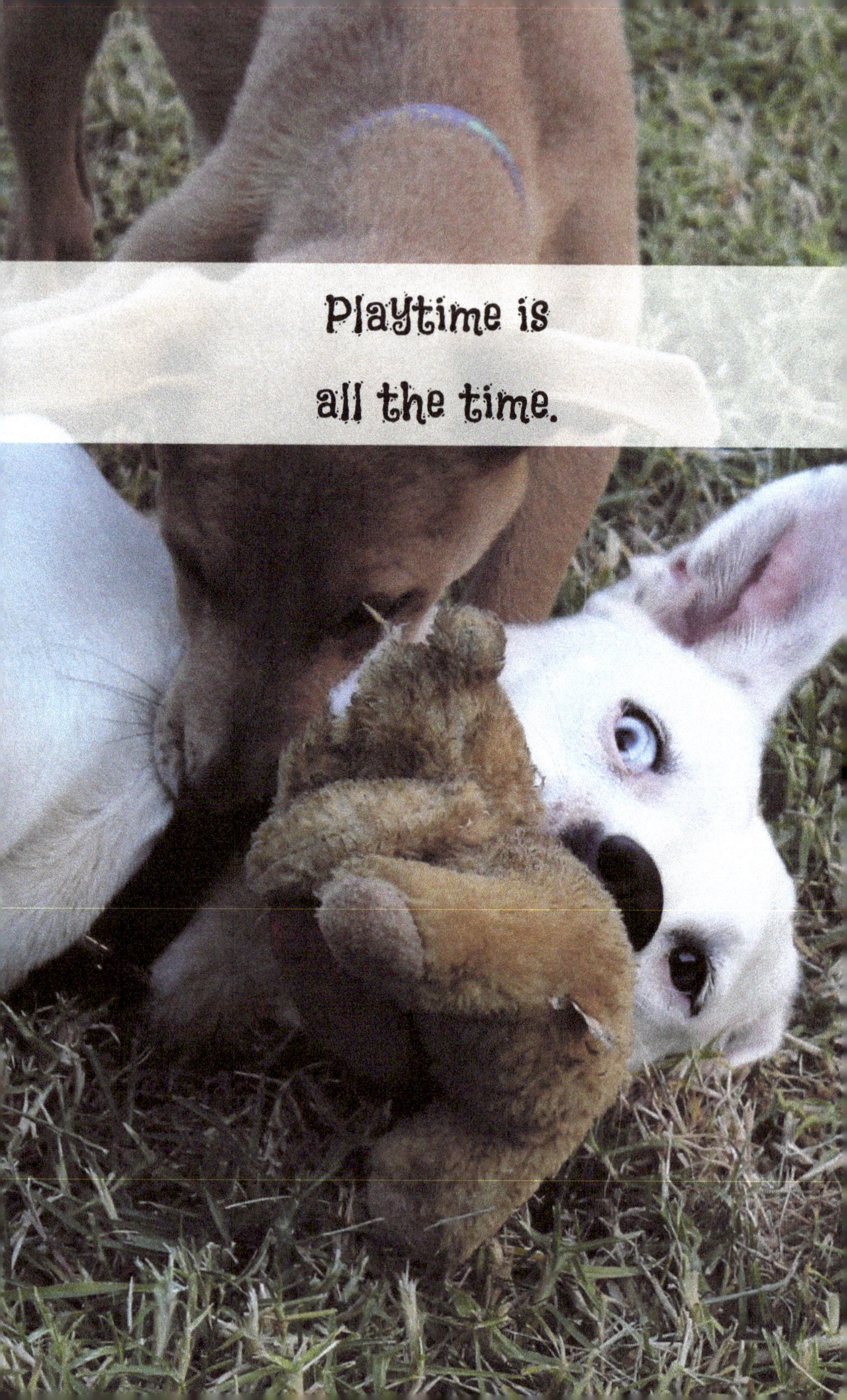
Playtime is
all the time.

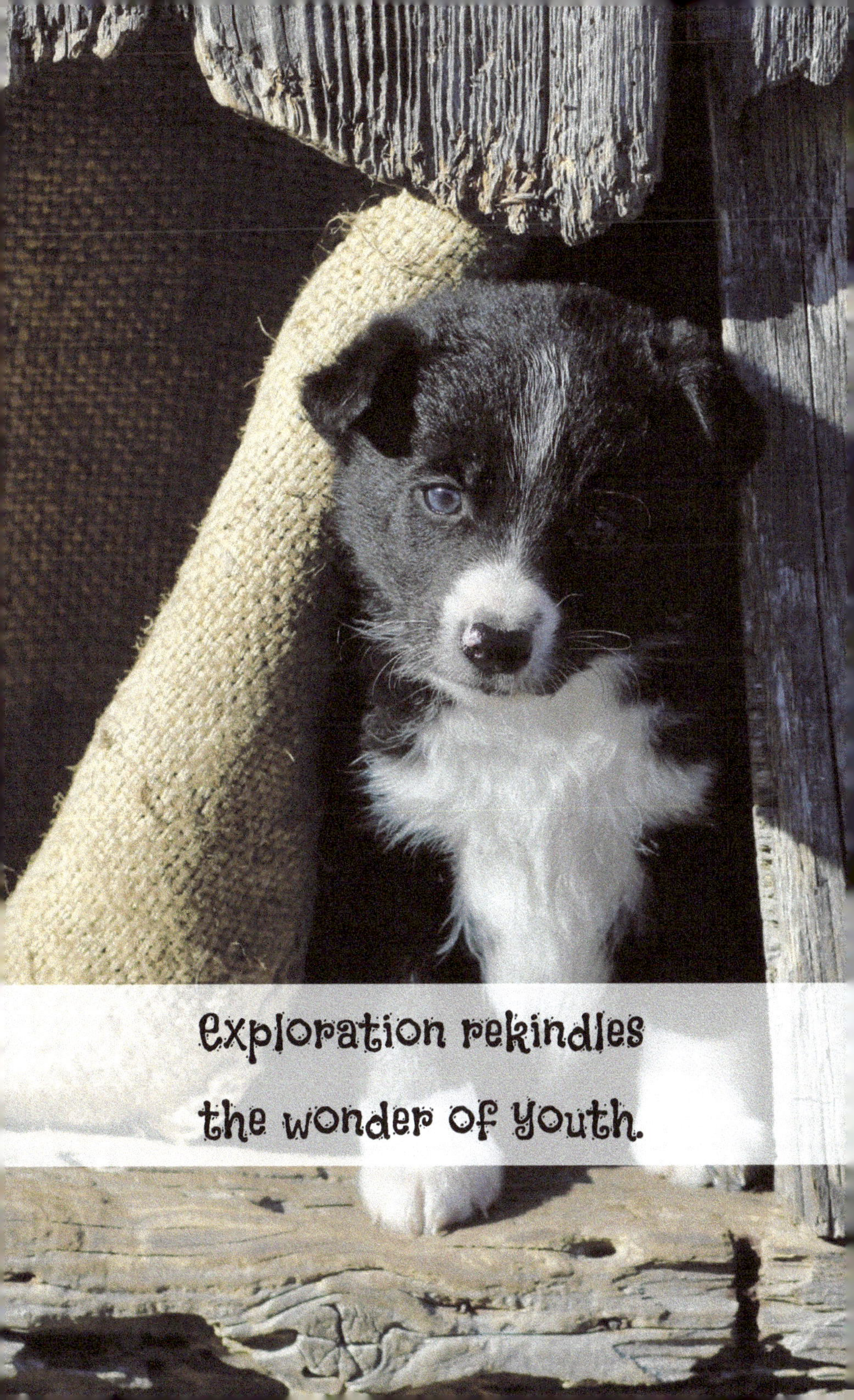

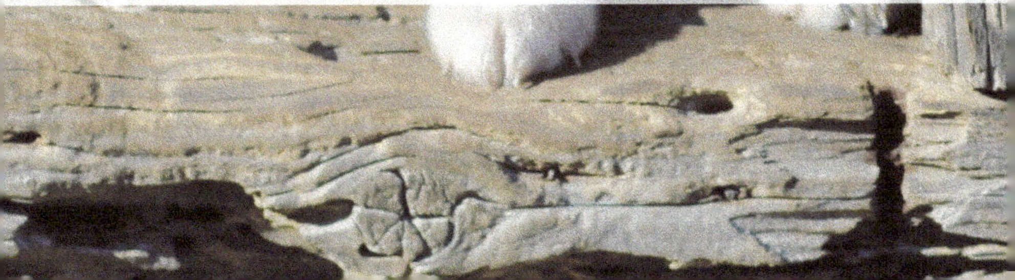

exploration rekindles
the wonder of youth.

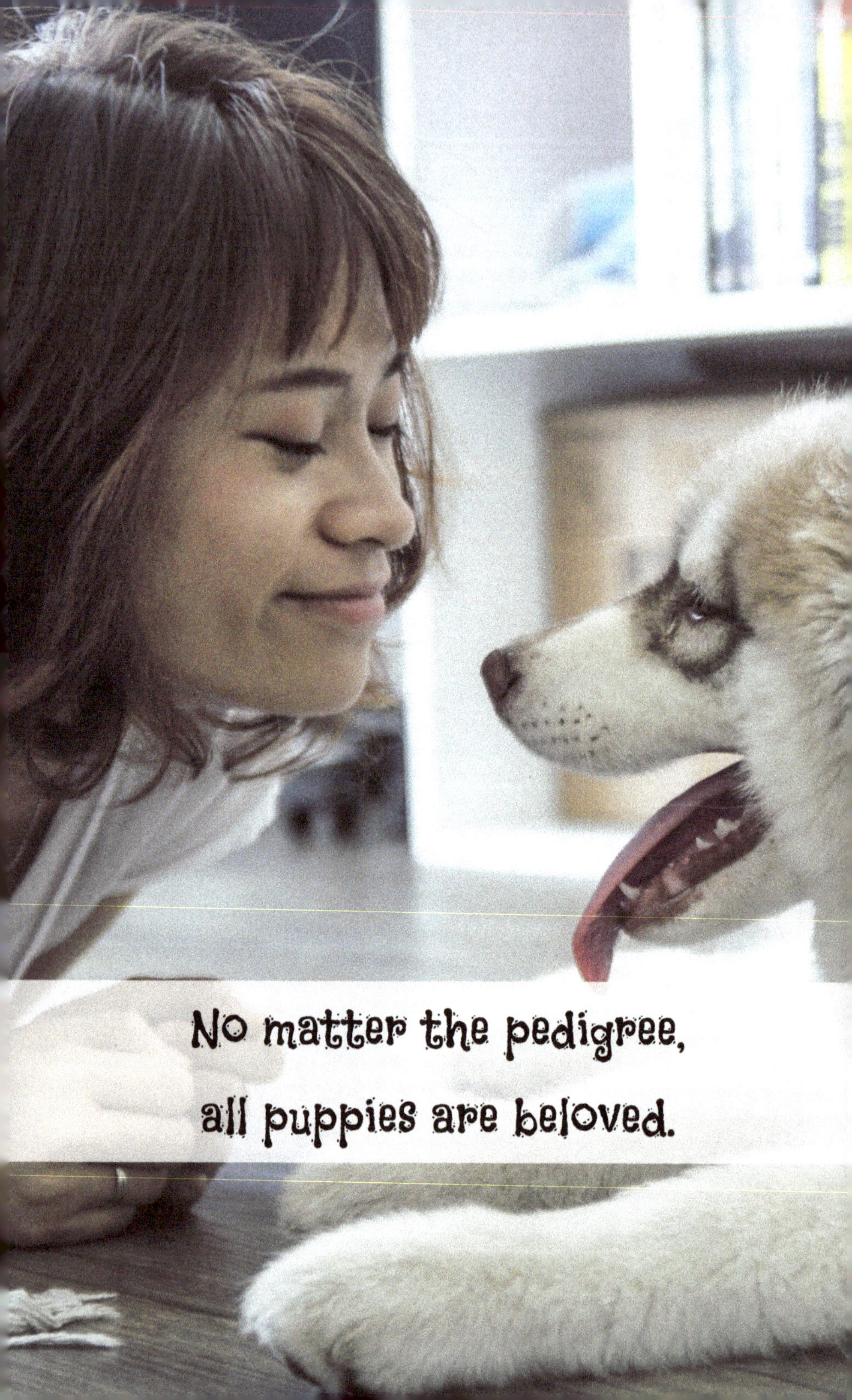
No matter the pedigree,
all puppies are beloved.

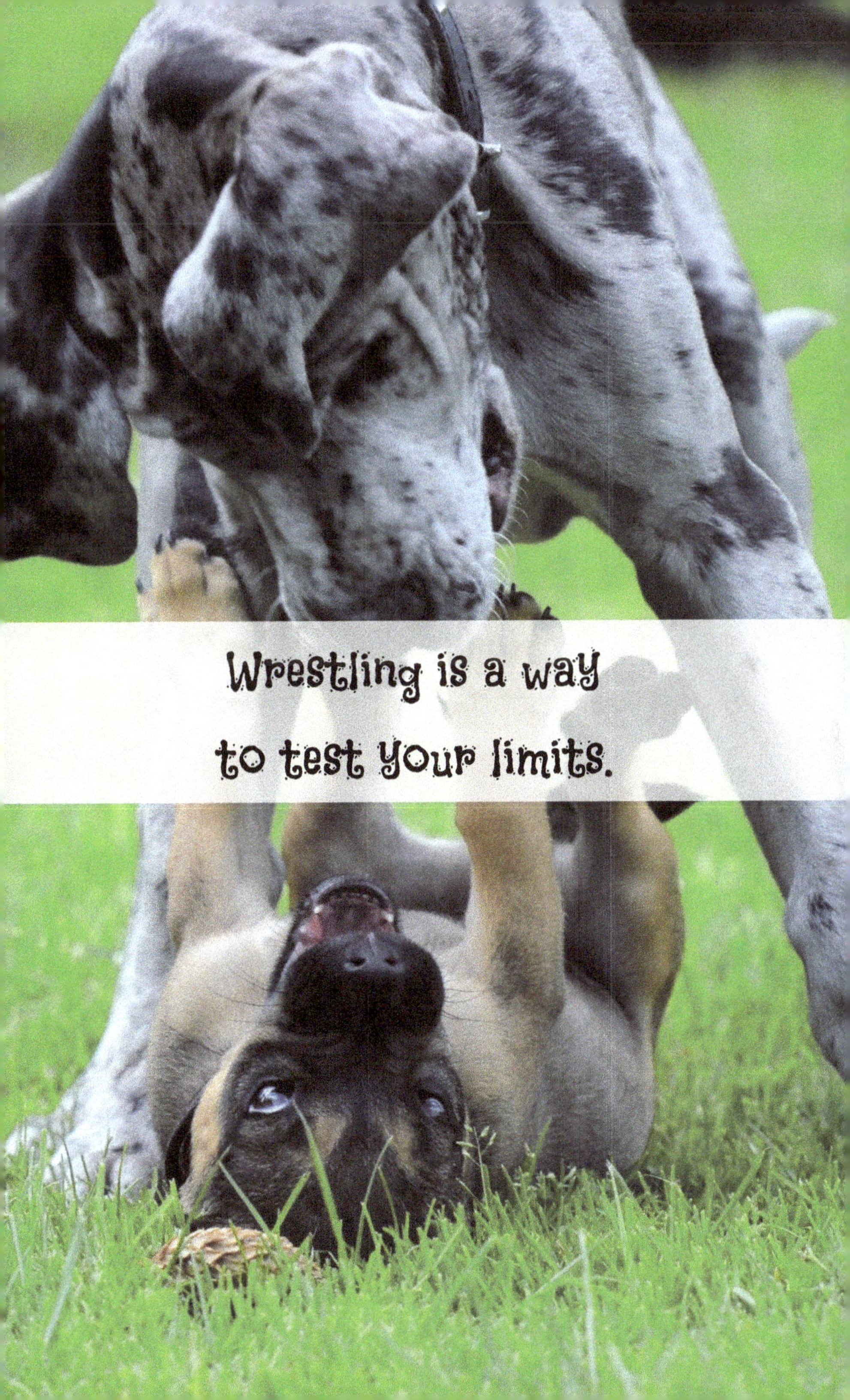

Wrestling is a way
to test your limits.

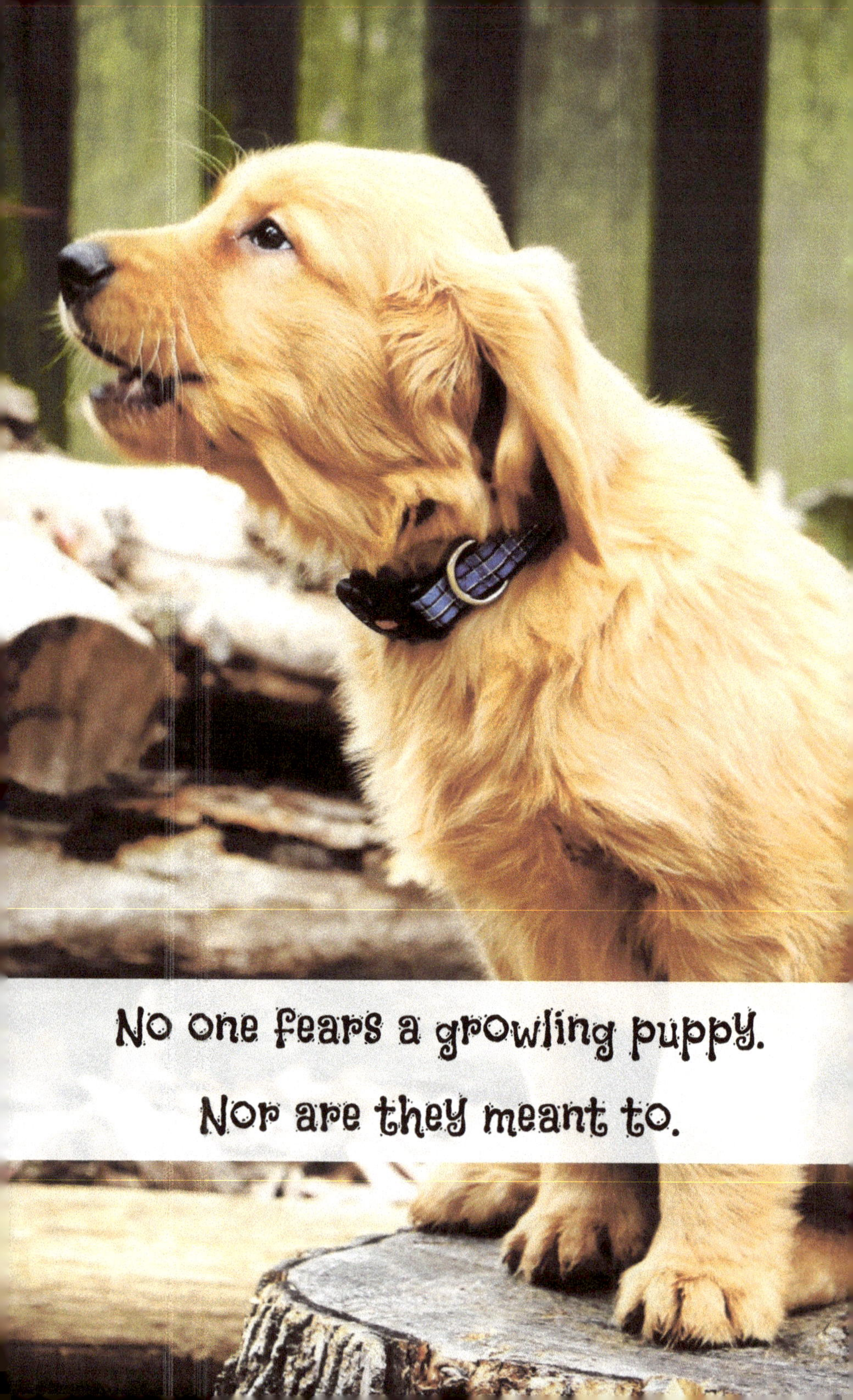

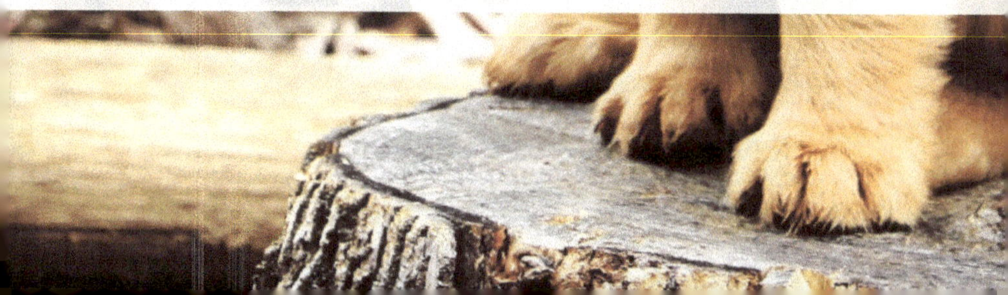

No one fears a growling puppy.
Nor are they meant to.

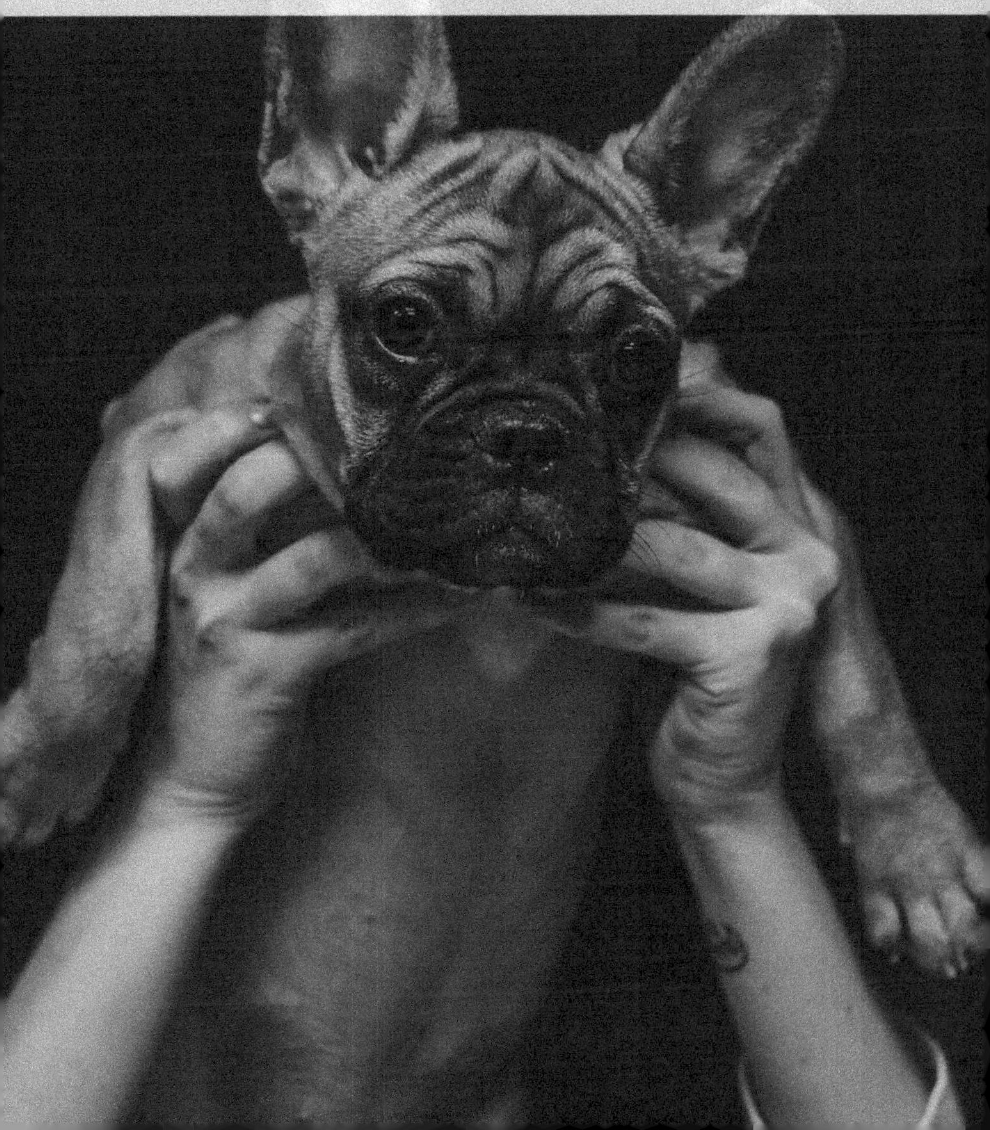

A trusting nature fuels

a loving soul.

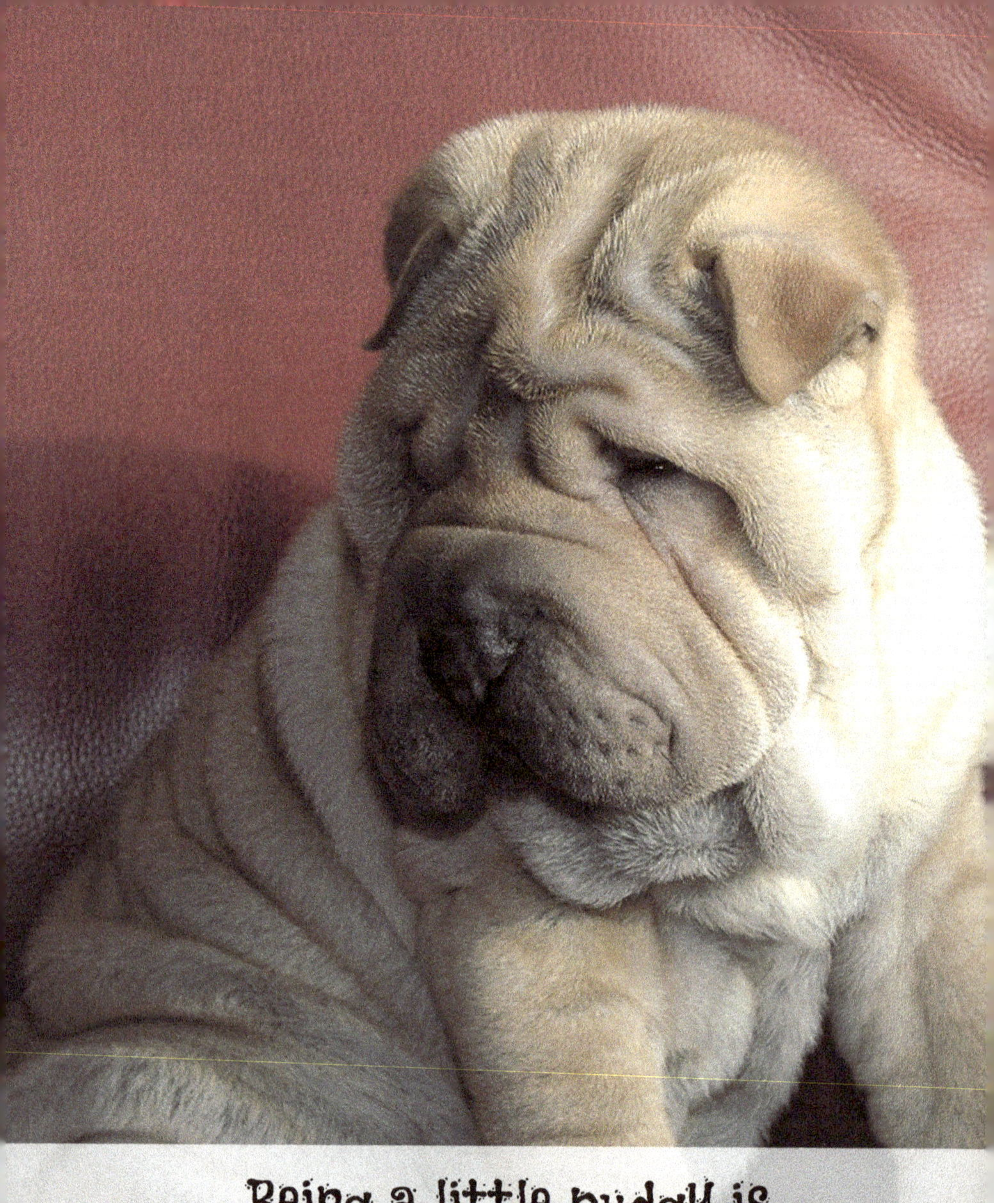
Being a little pudgy is
a sign of good health.

Puppies never change their spots
but they might change their color.

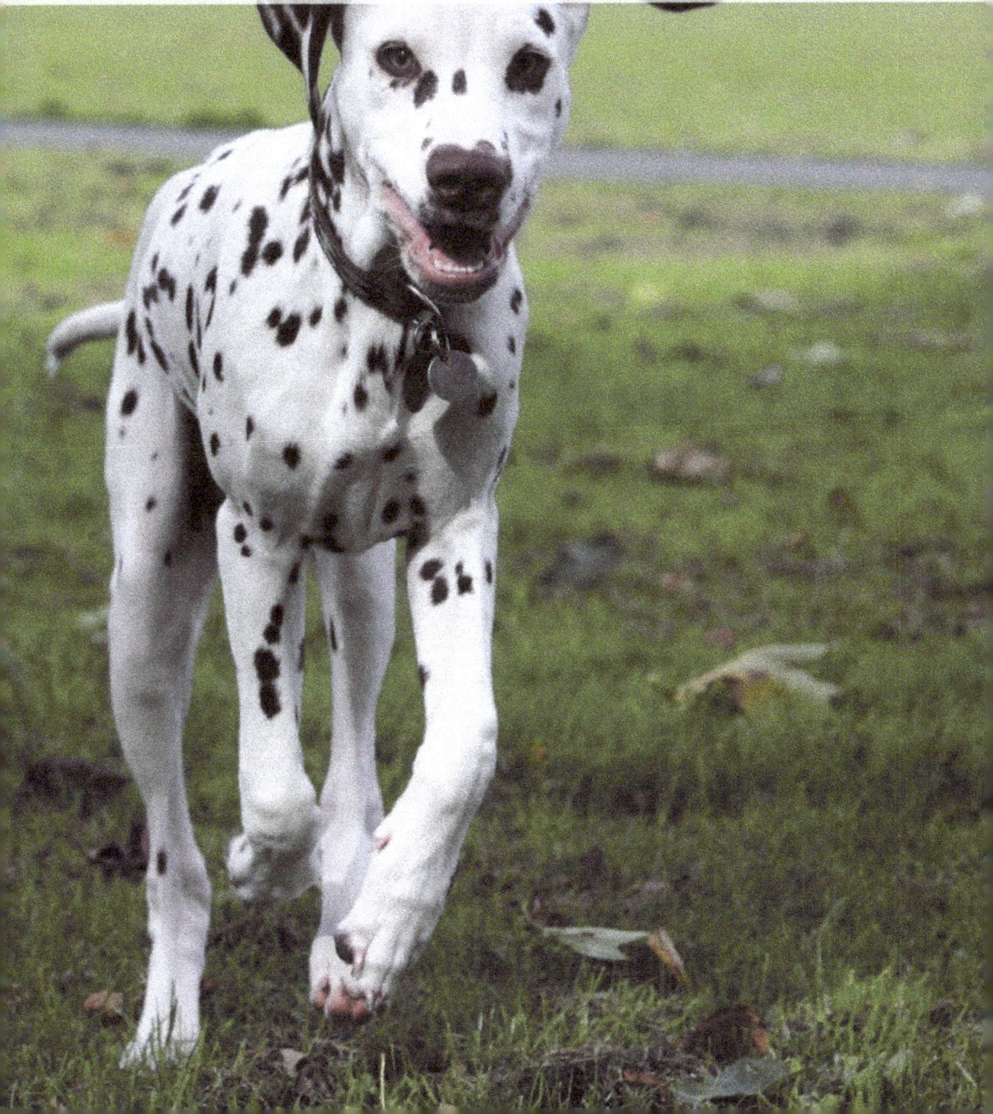

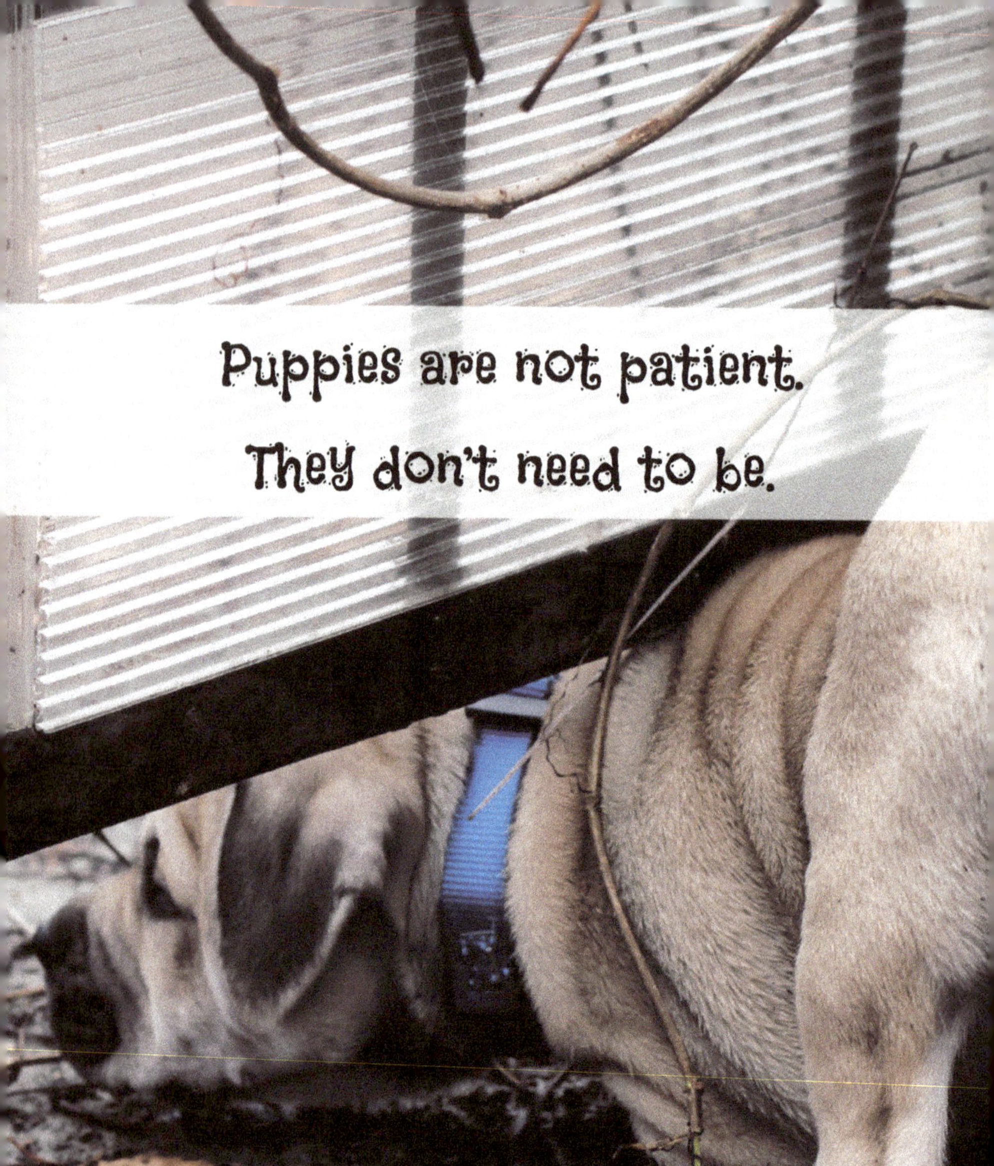

Puppies are not patient.
They don't need to be.

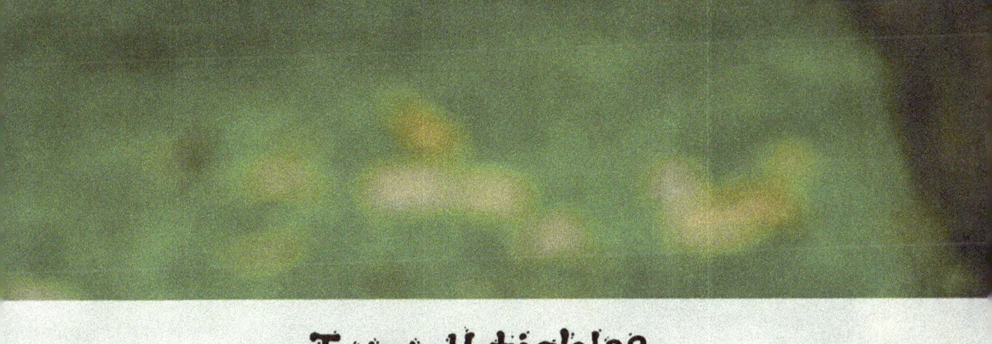

Tummy tickles
are good for everyone.

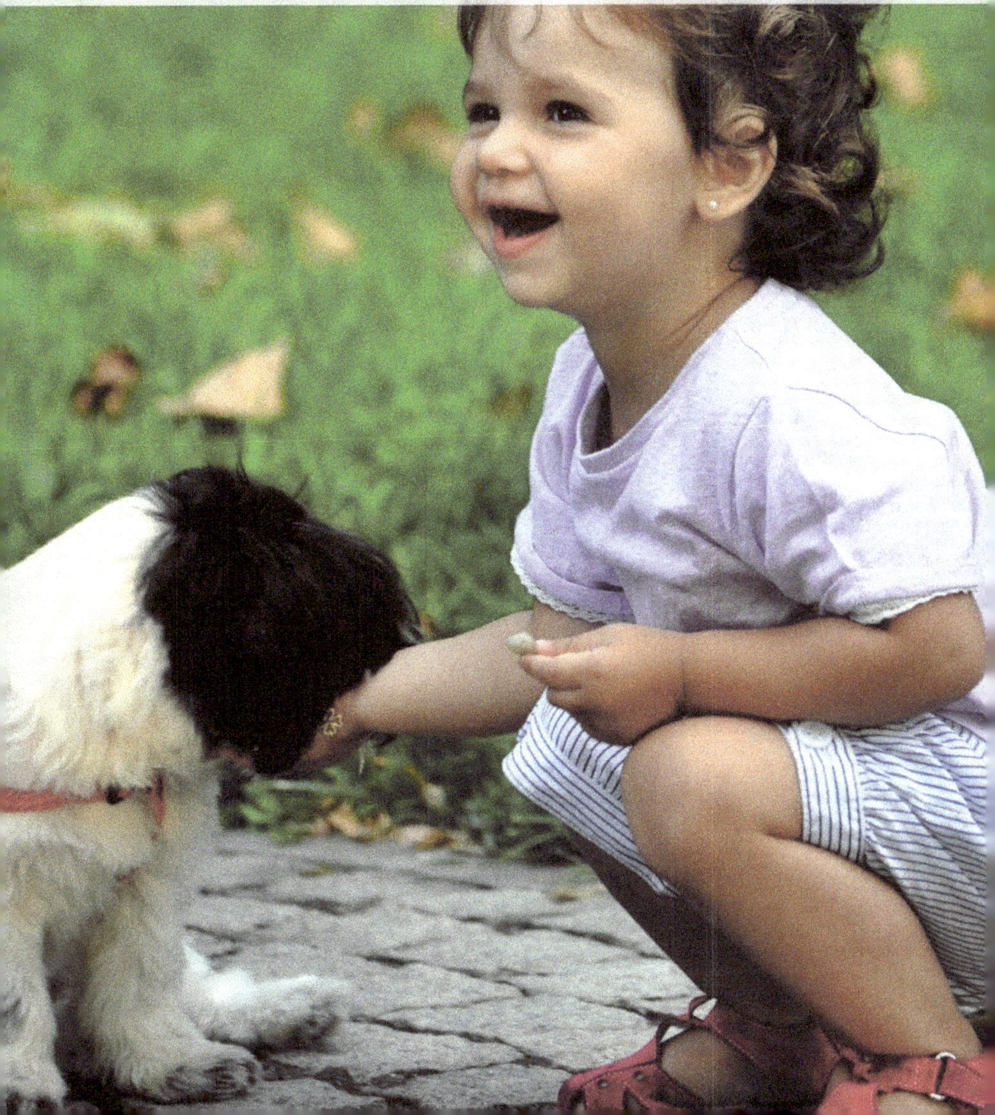

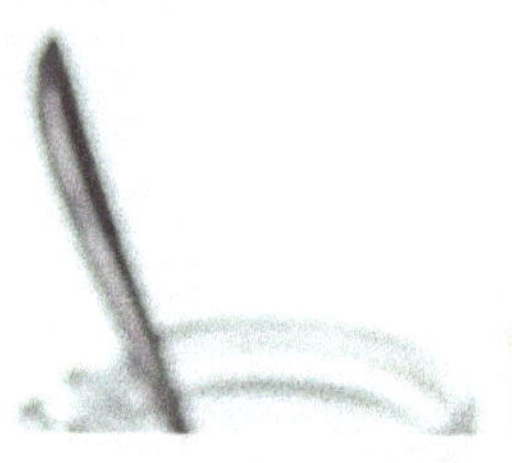

The clumsiest puppy
is a ninja in its mind.

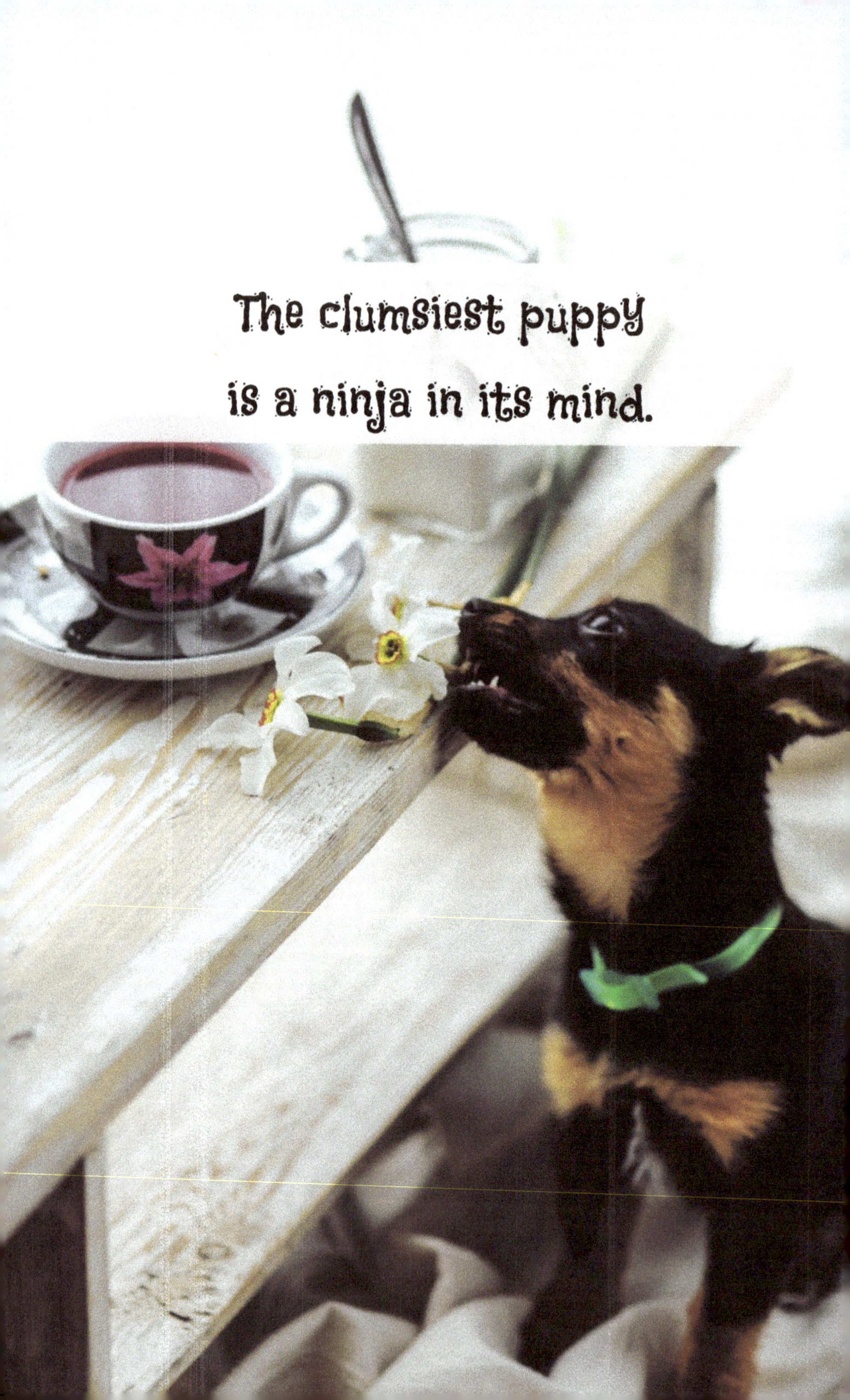

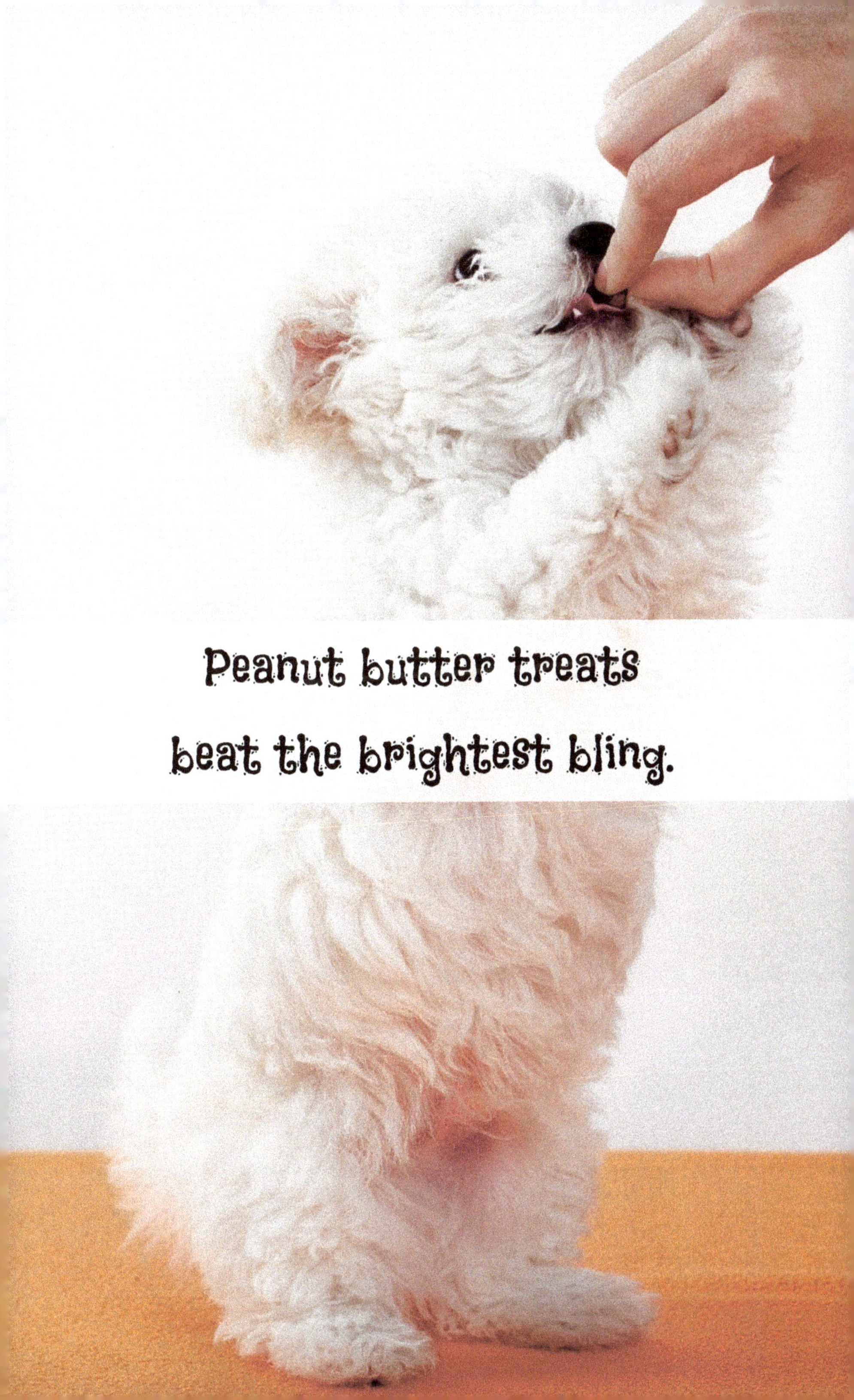

Peanut butter treats
beat the brightest bling.

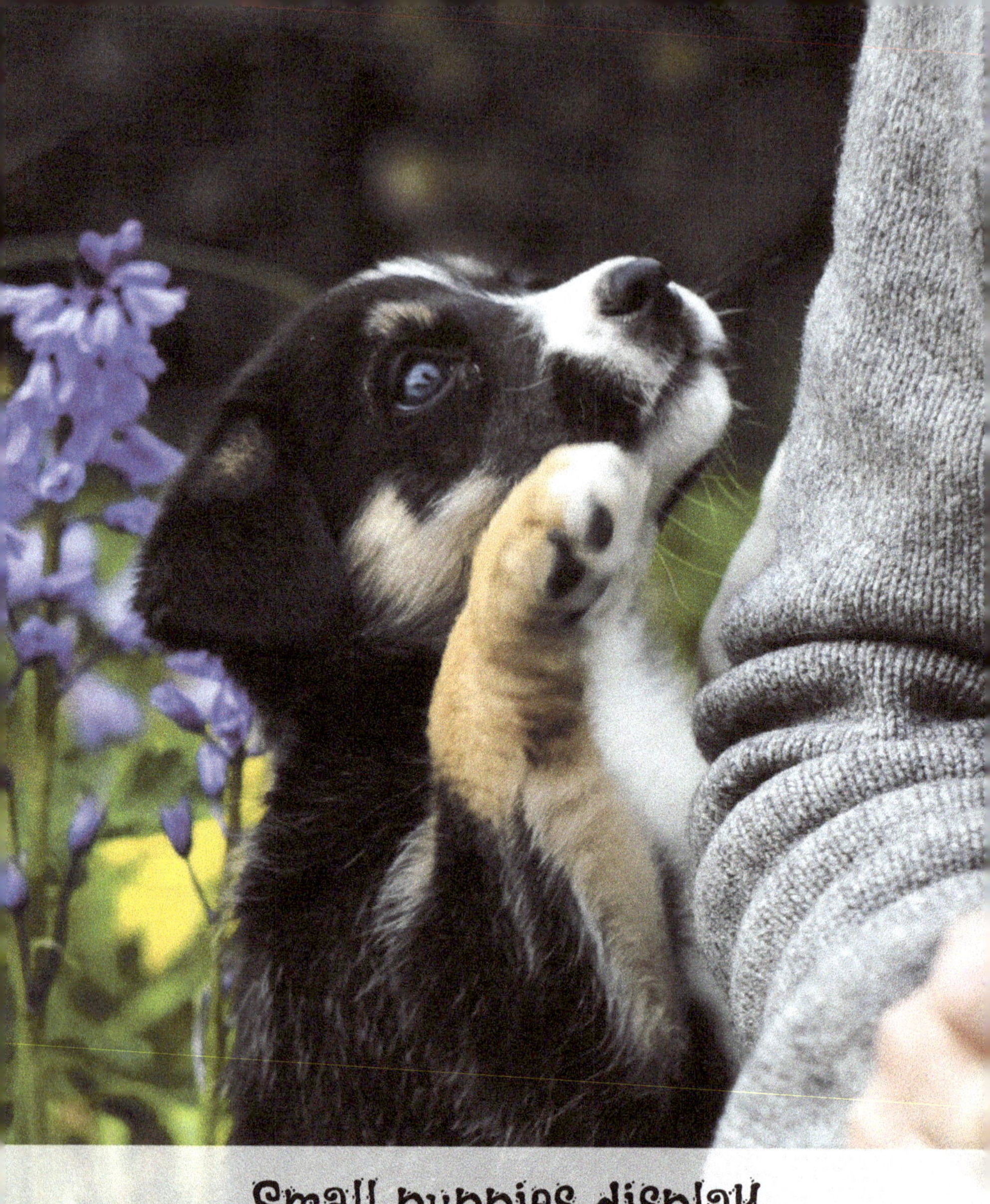

Small puppies display
large talents.

Chasing your tail is
ridiculously fun.

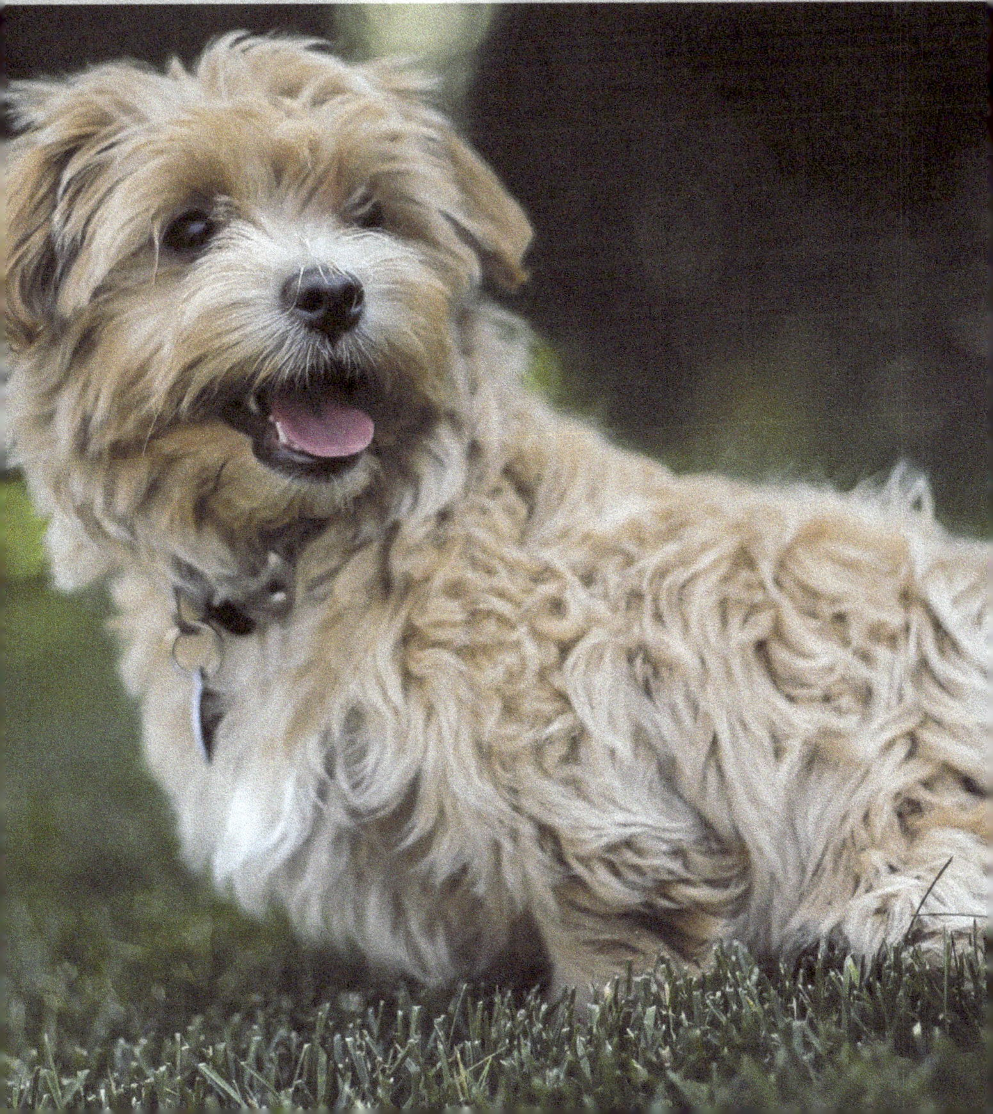

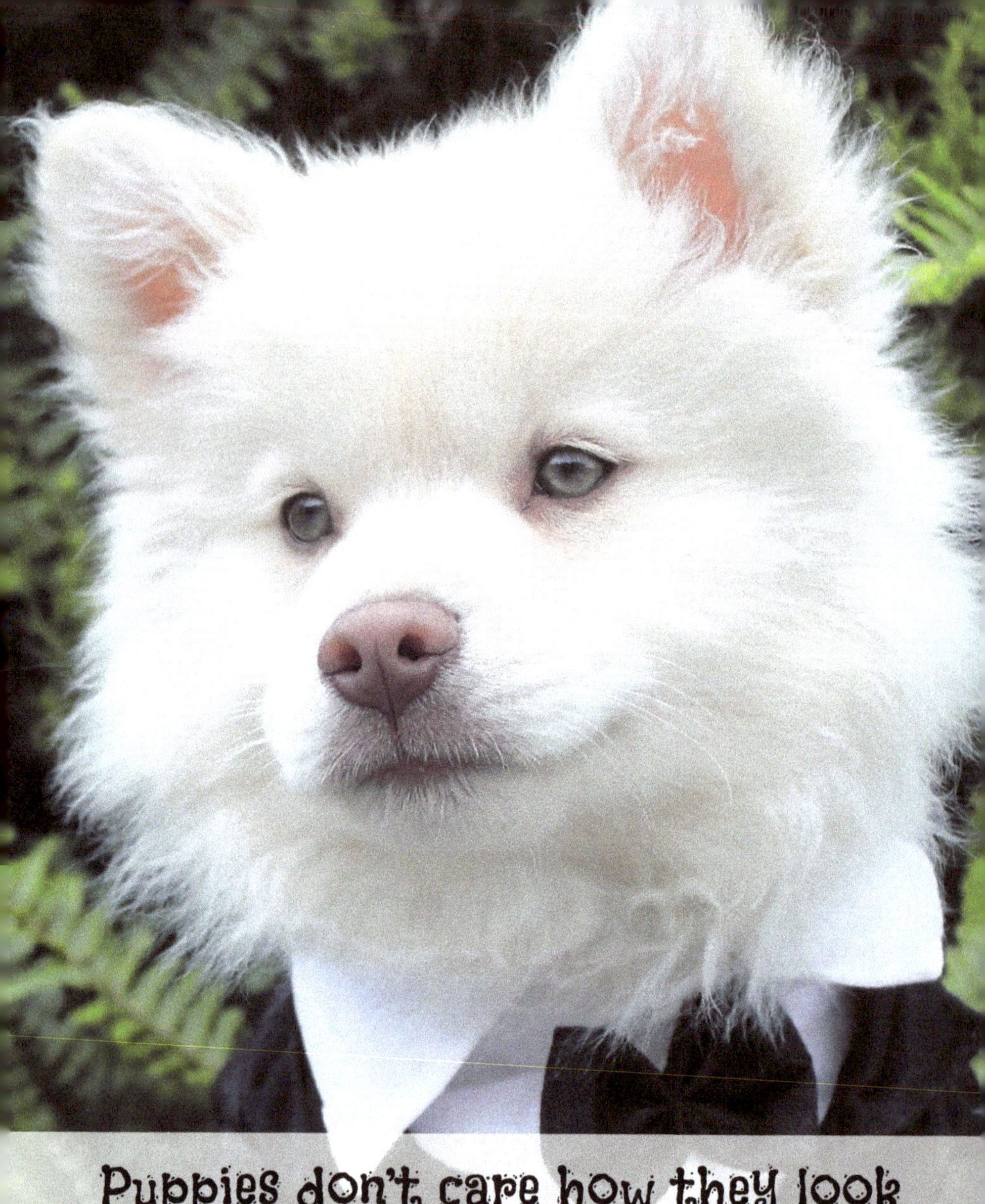
Puppies don't care how they look
They only care how they feel.

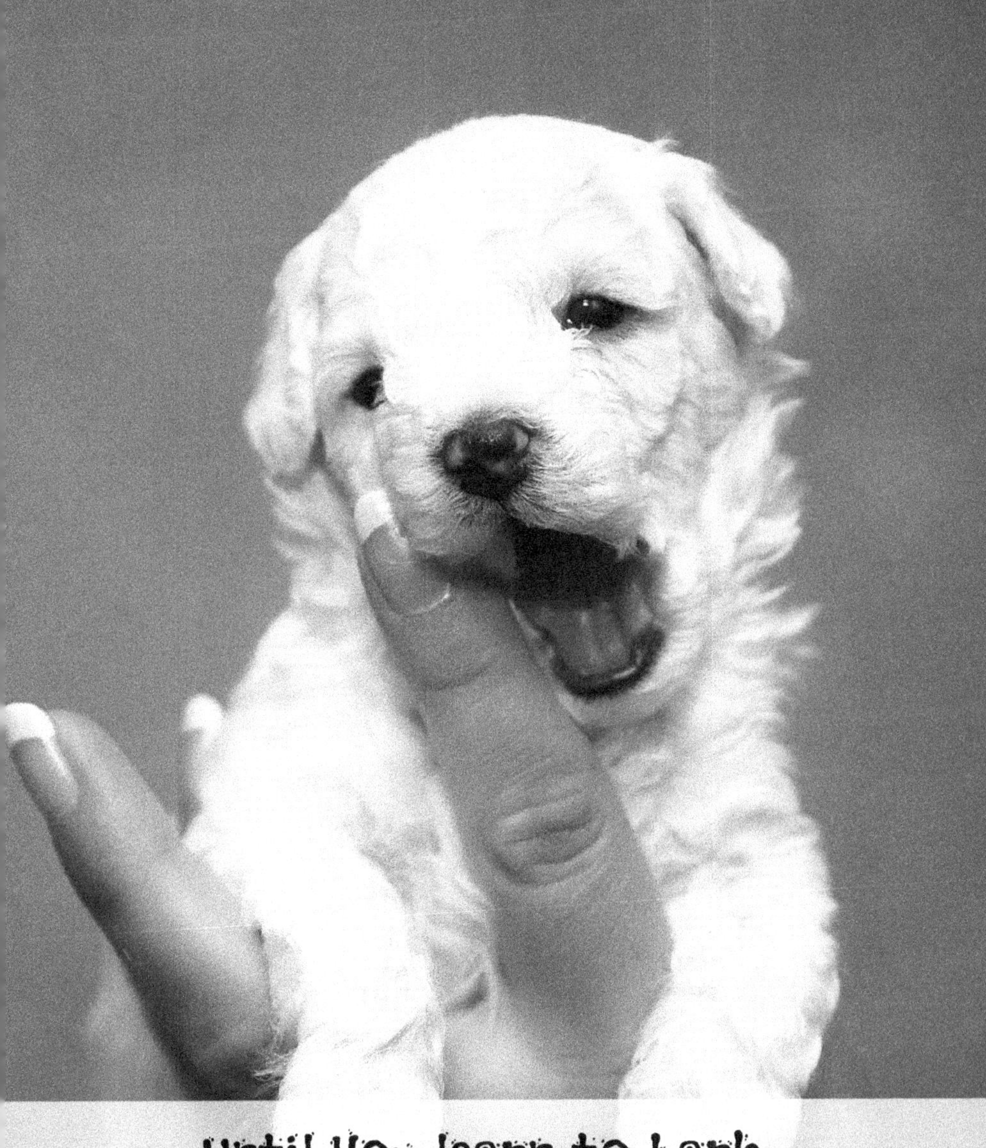
Until you learn to bark,
Yipping is just fine.

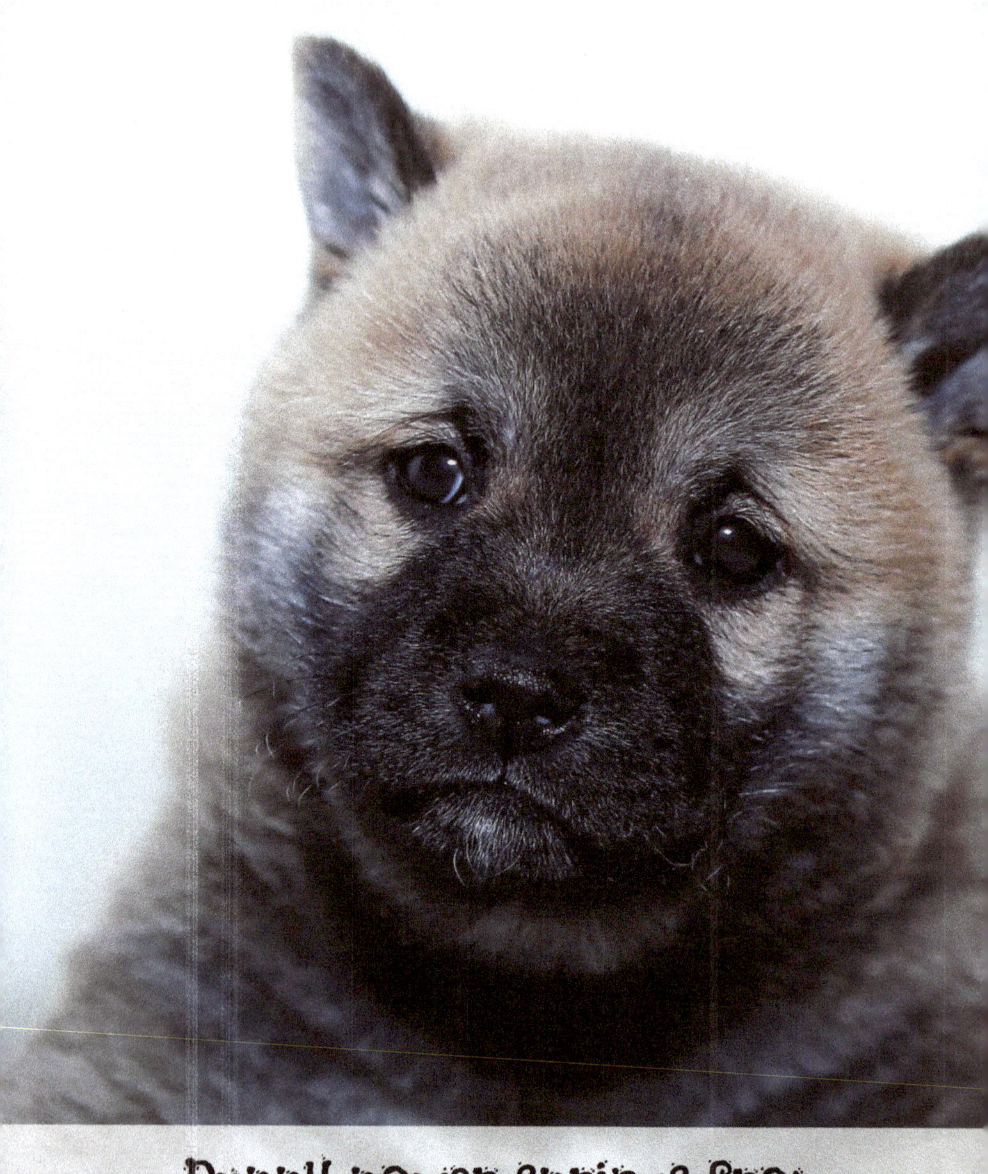

Puppy power springs from
touching hearts.

It's good to be distracted by
the bright and shining world.

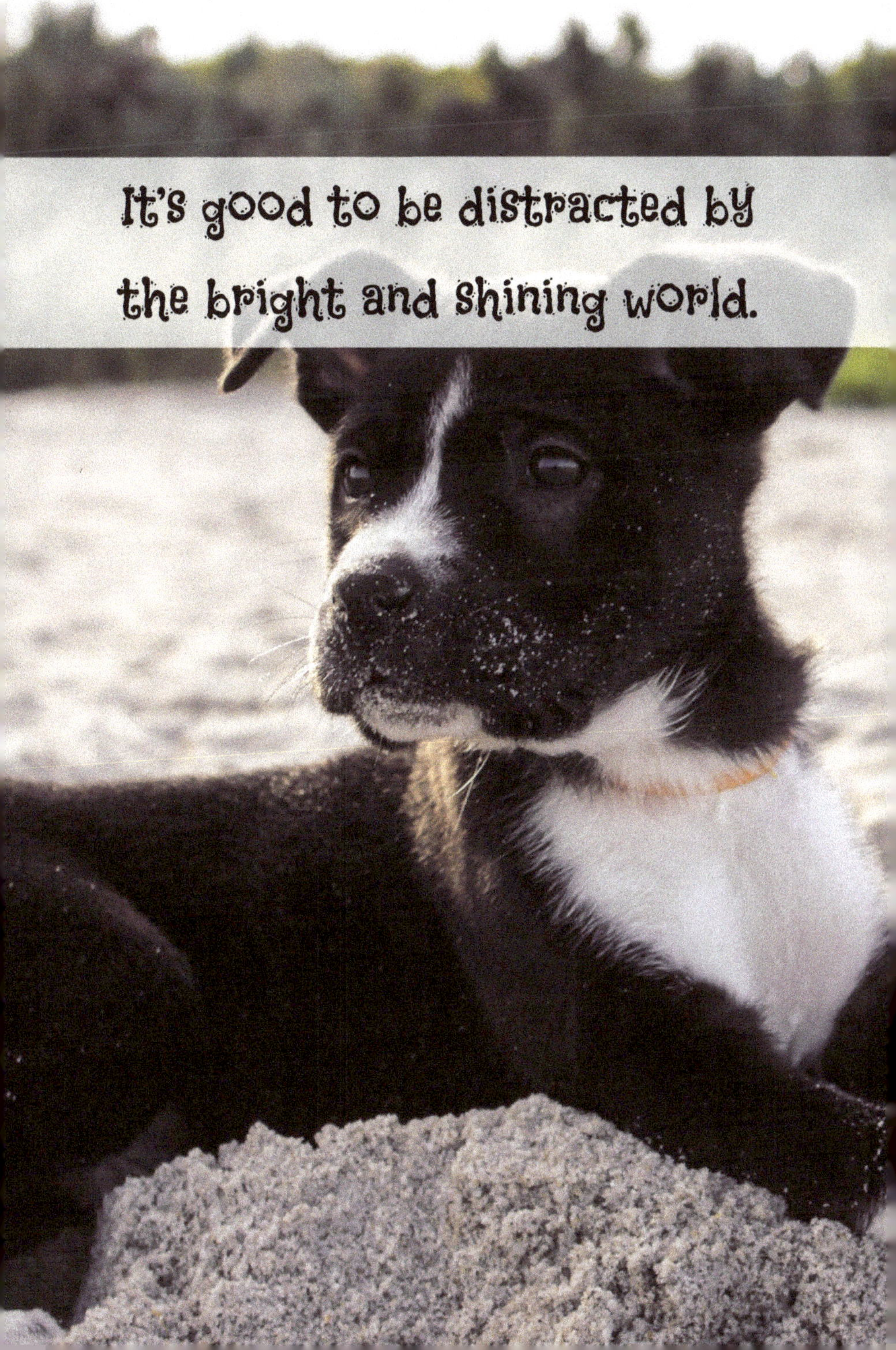

A pile of puppies is
a pile of love.

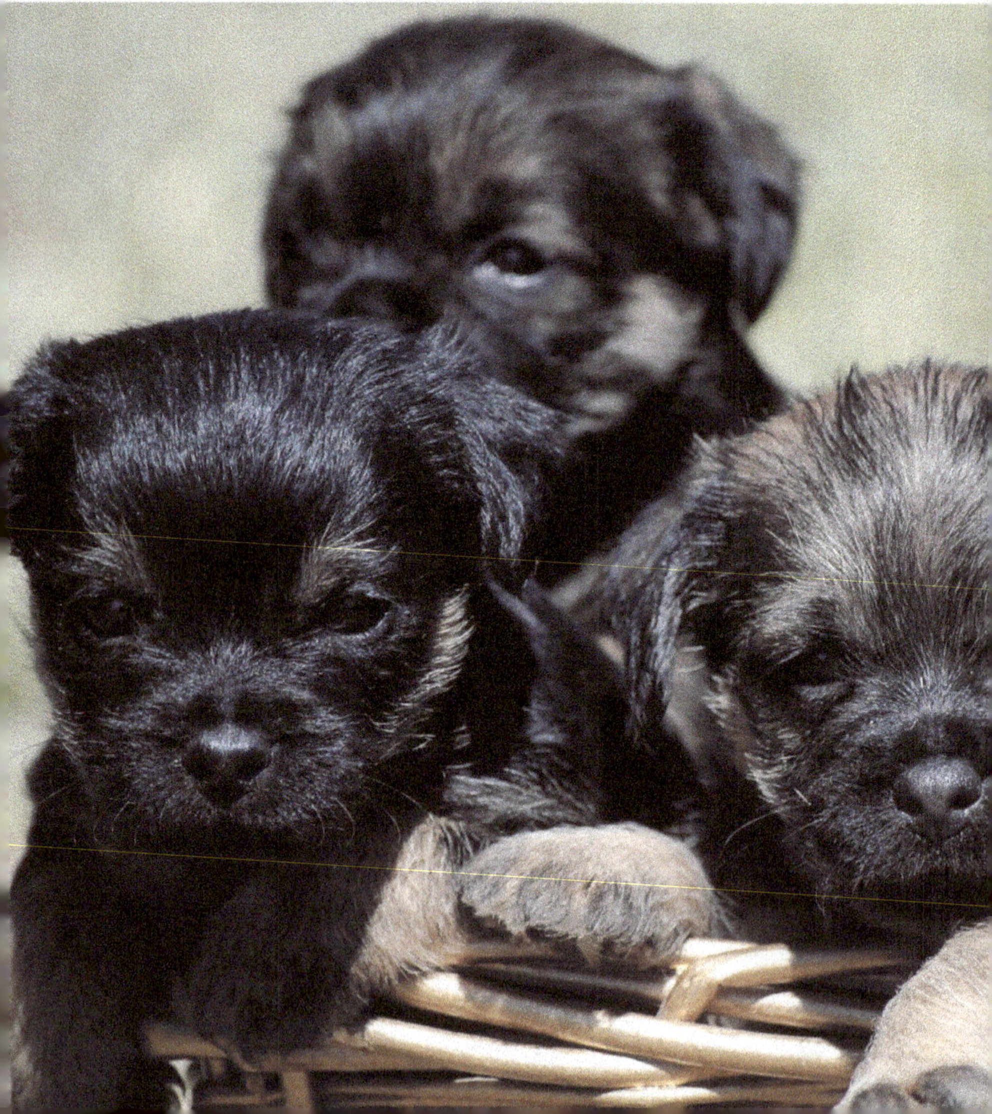

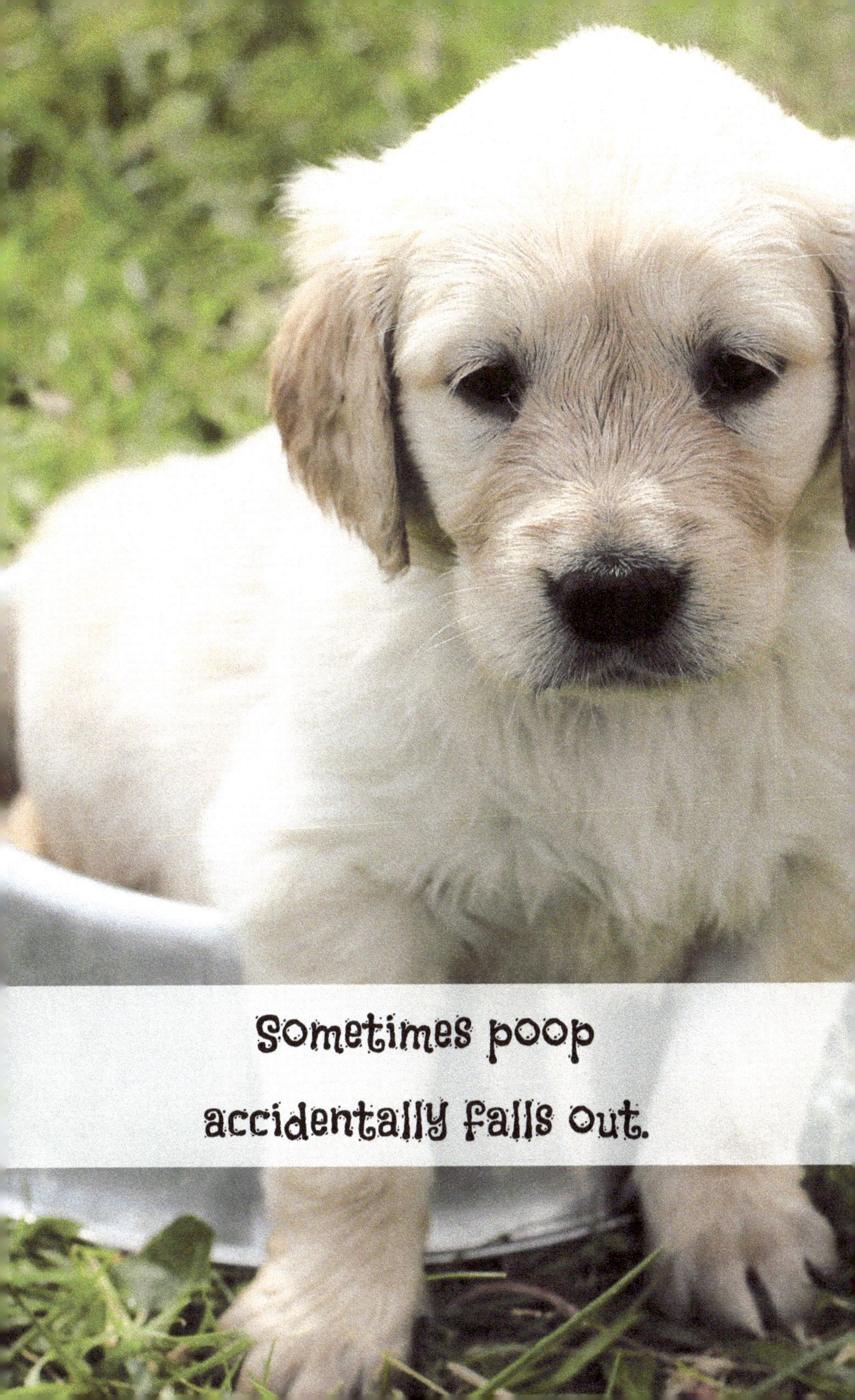

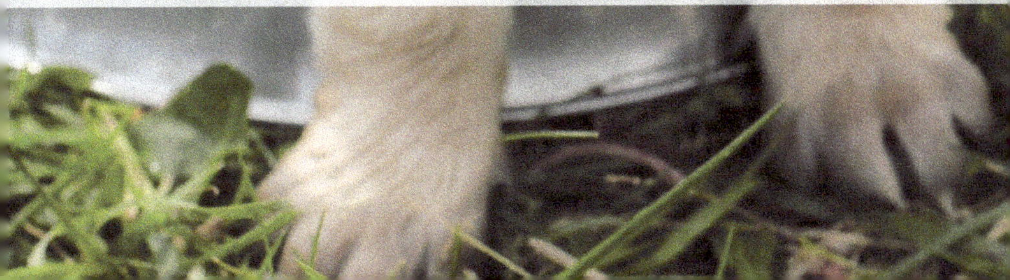

Sometimes poop
accidentally falls out.

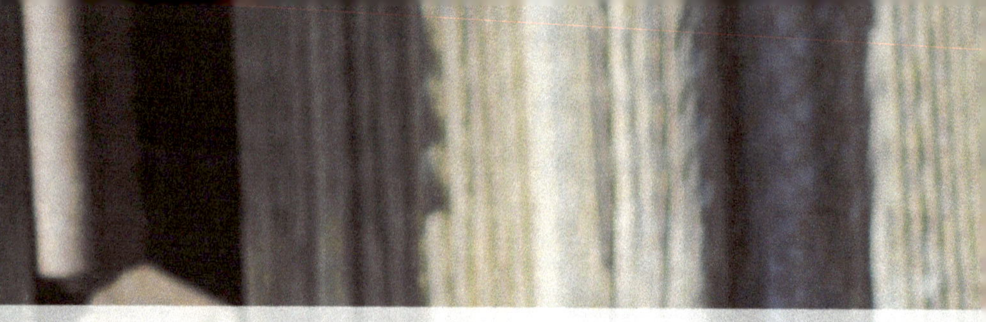
Falls, trips and stumbles
don't hurt a bit.

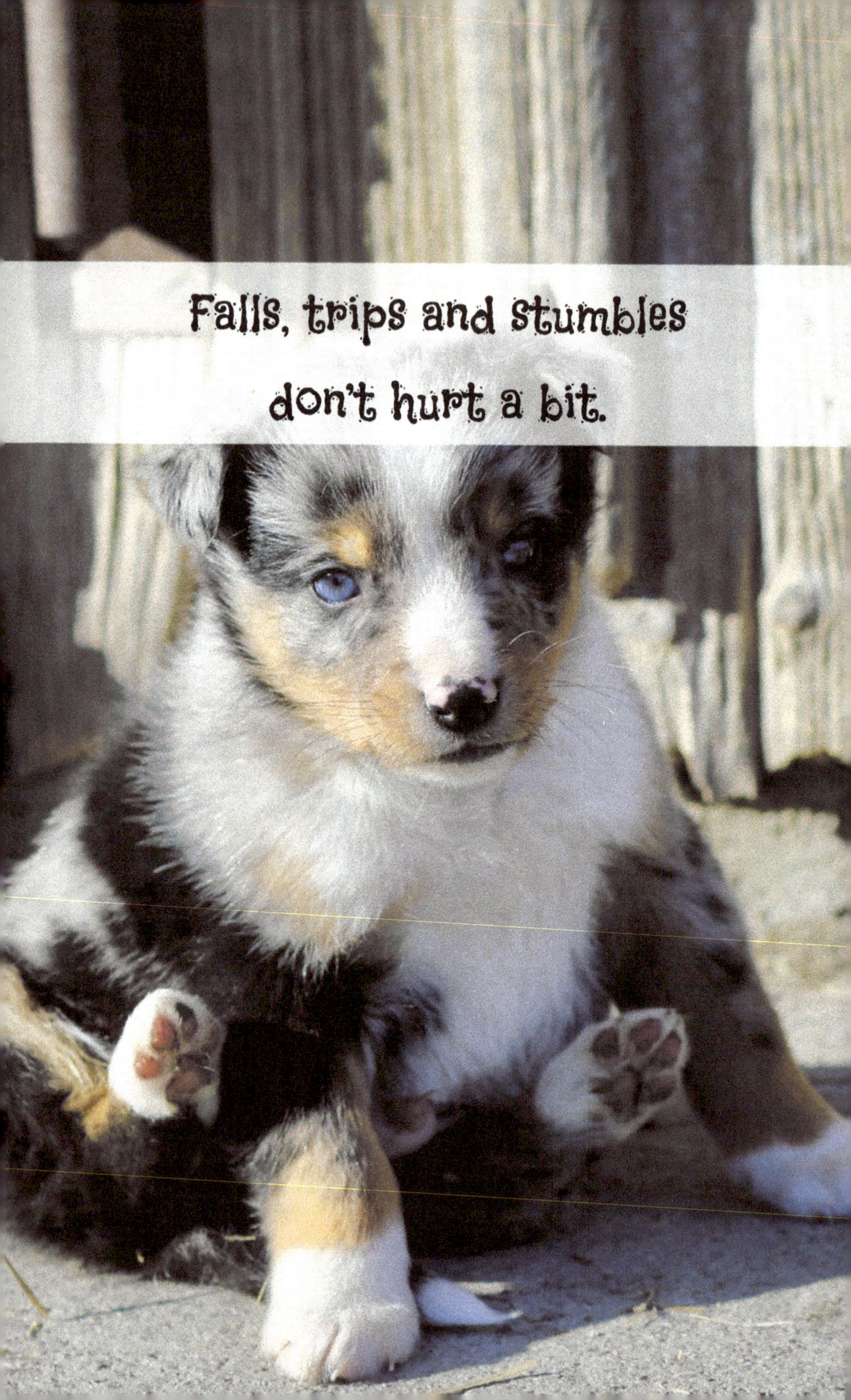

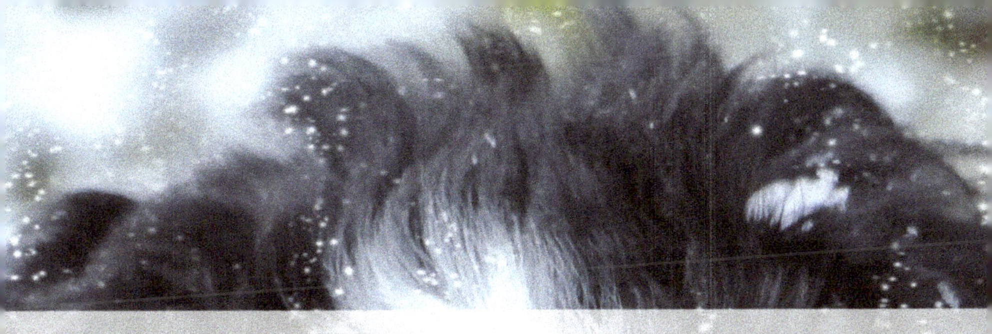

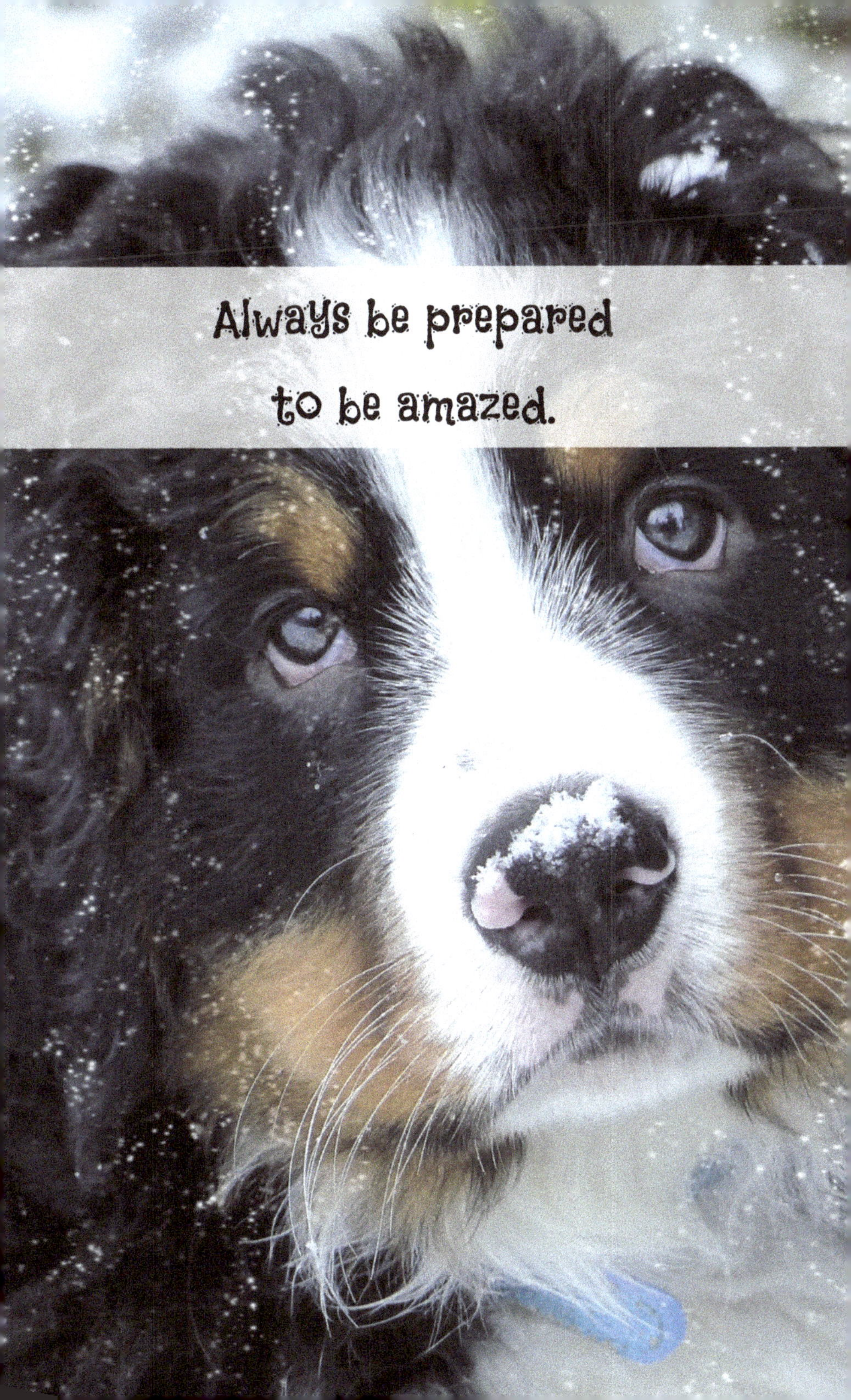

Always be prepared
to be amazed.

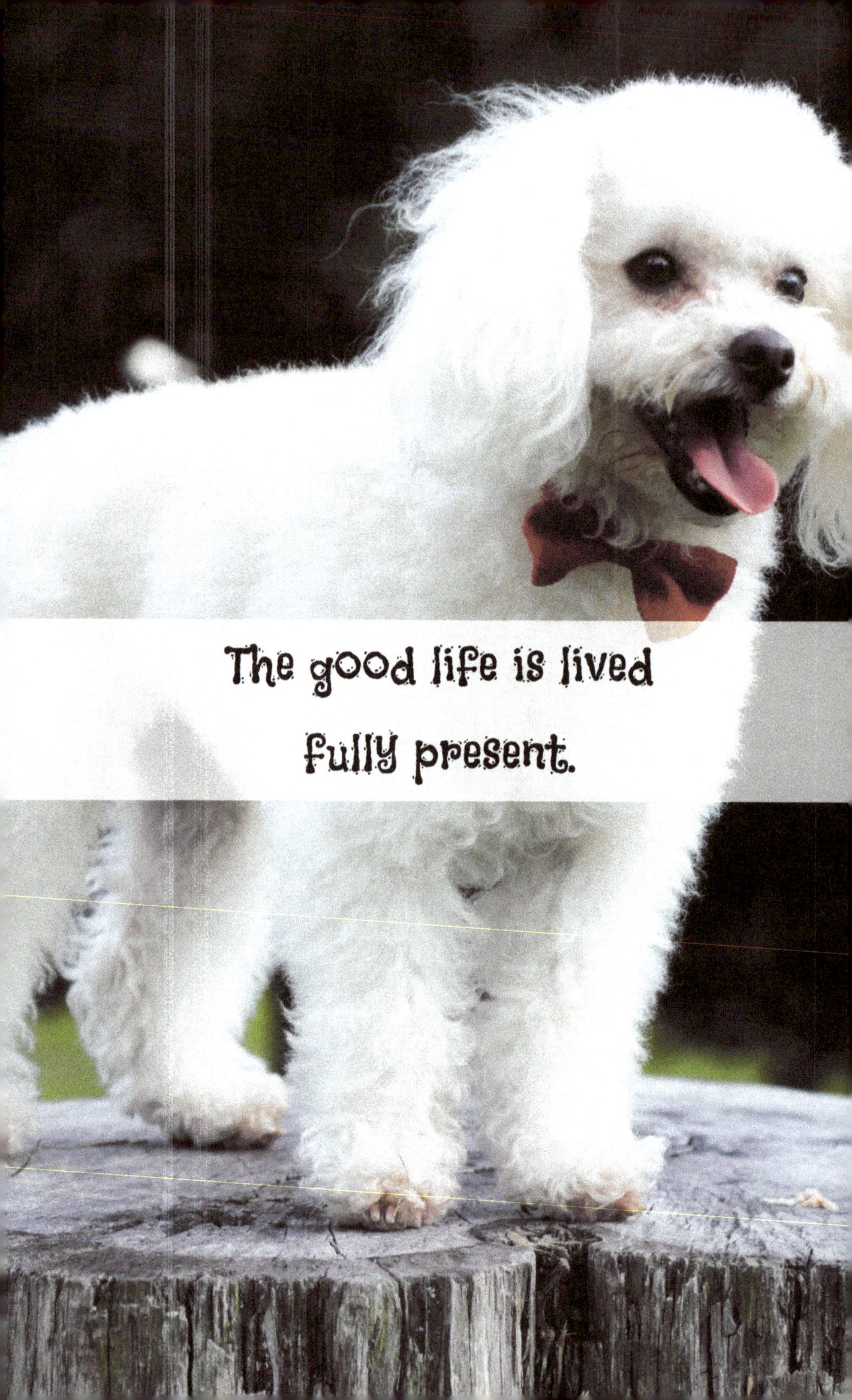

The good life is lived
fully present.

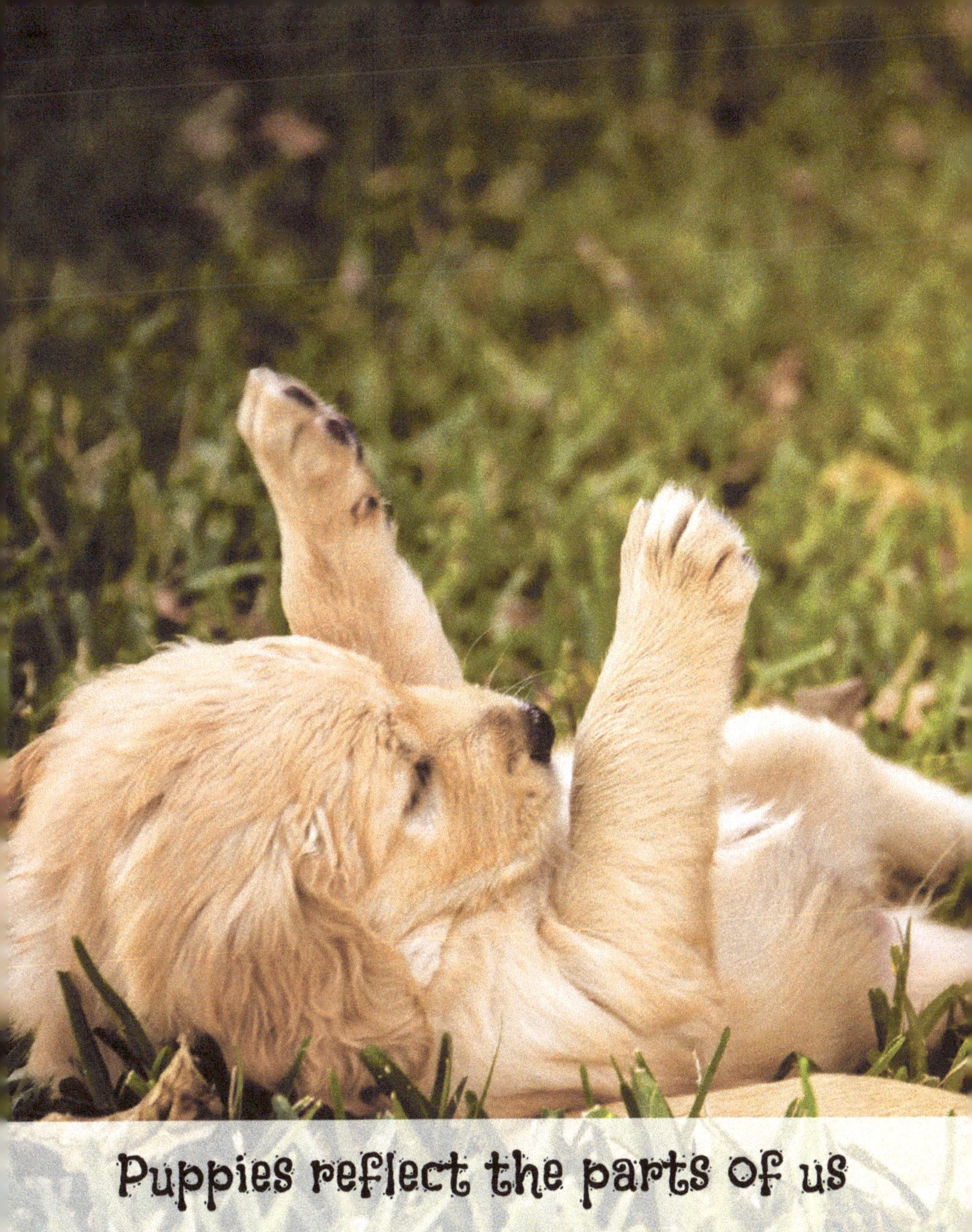

Puppies reflect the parts of us
that deserve to be loved.

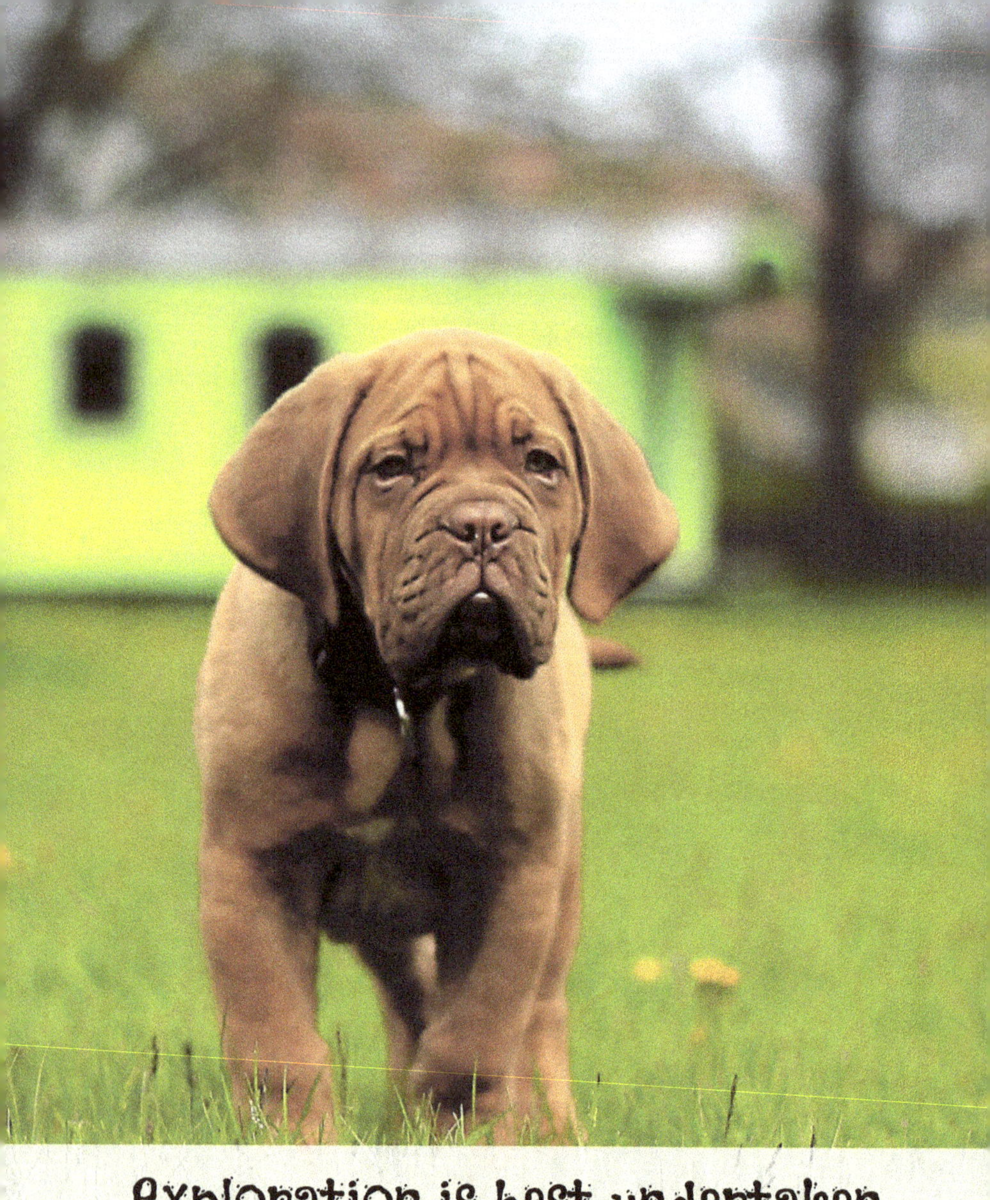

exploration is best undertaken
without preconceived limits.

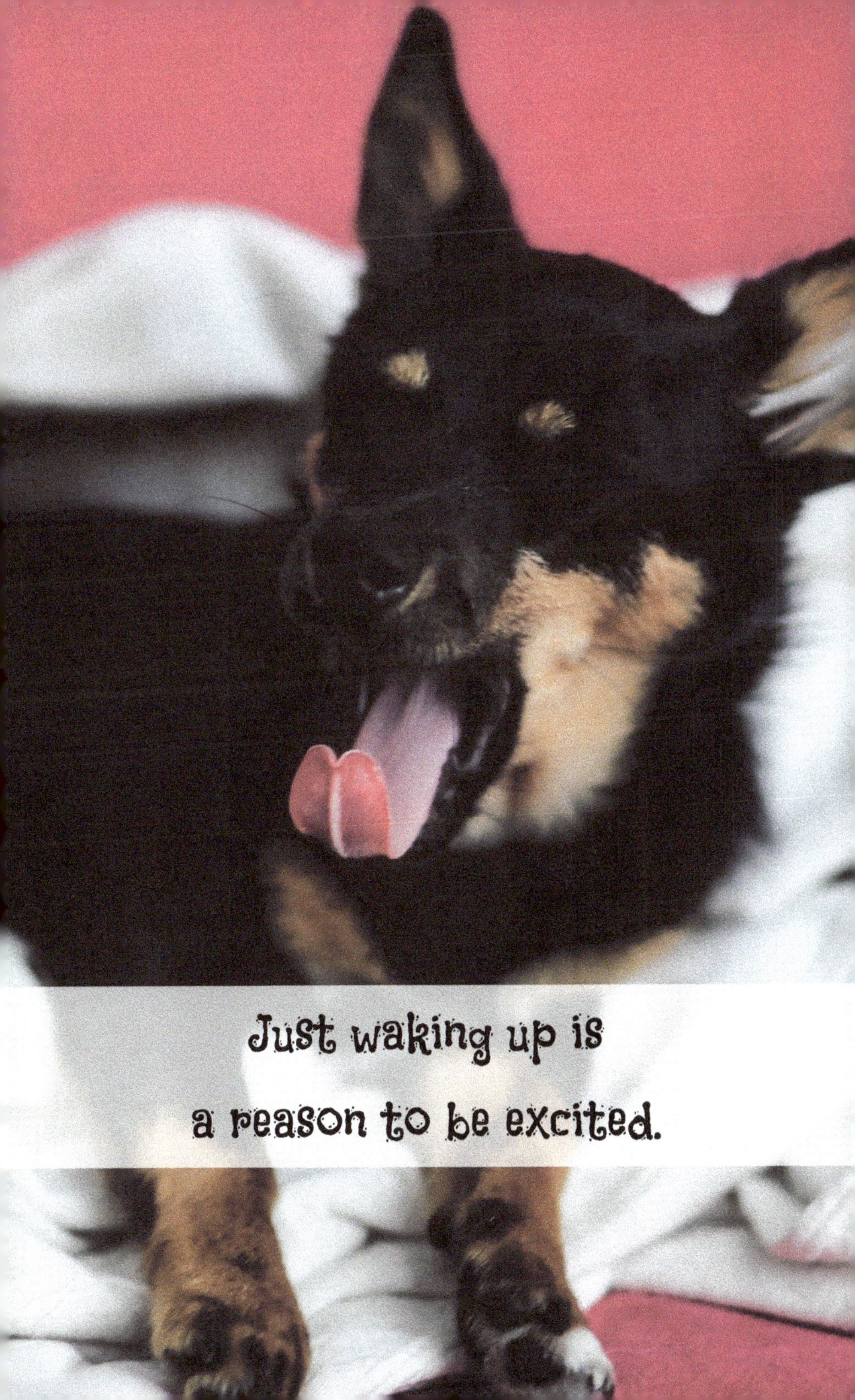

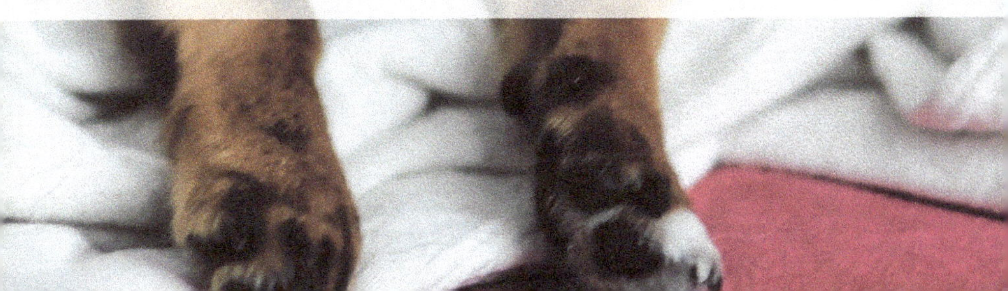

Just waking up is
a reason to be excited.

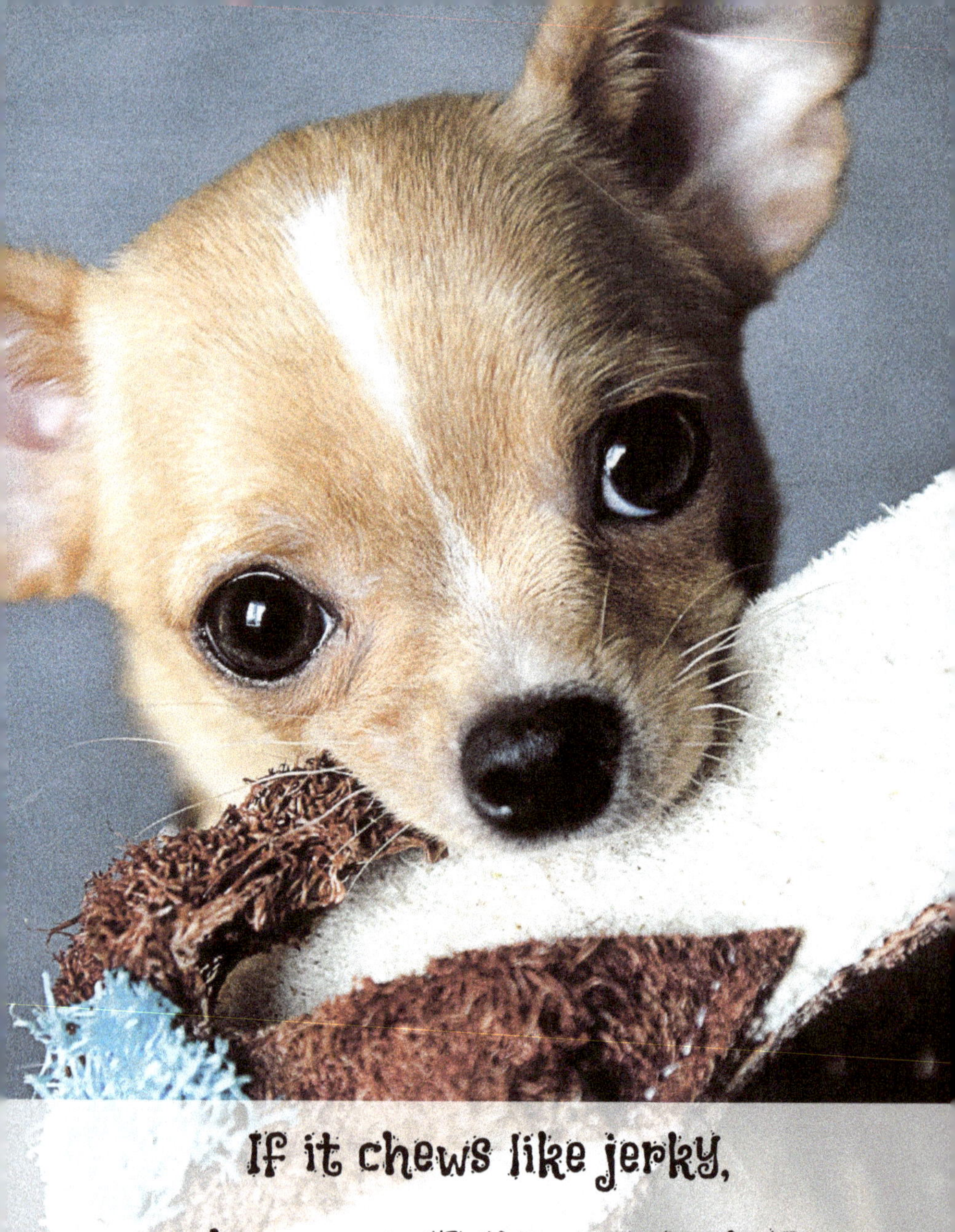
If it chews like jerky,
who cares if it's not jerky?

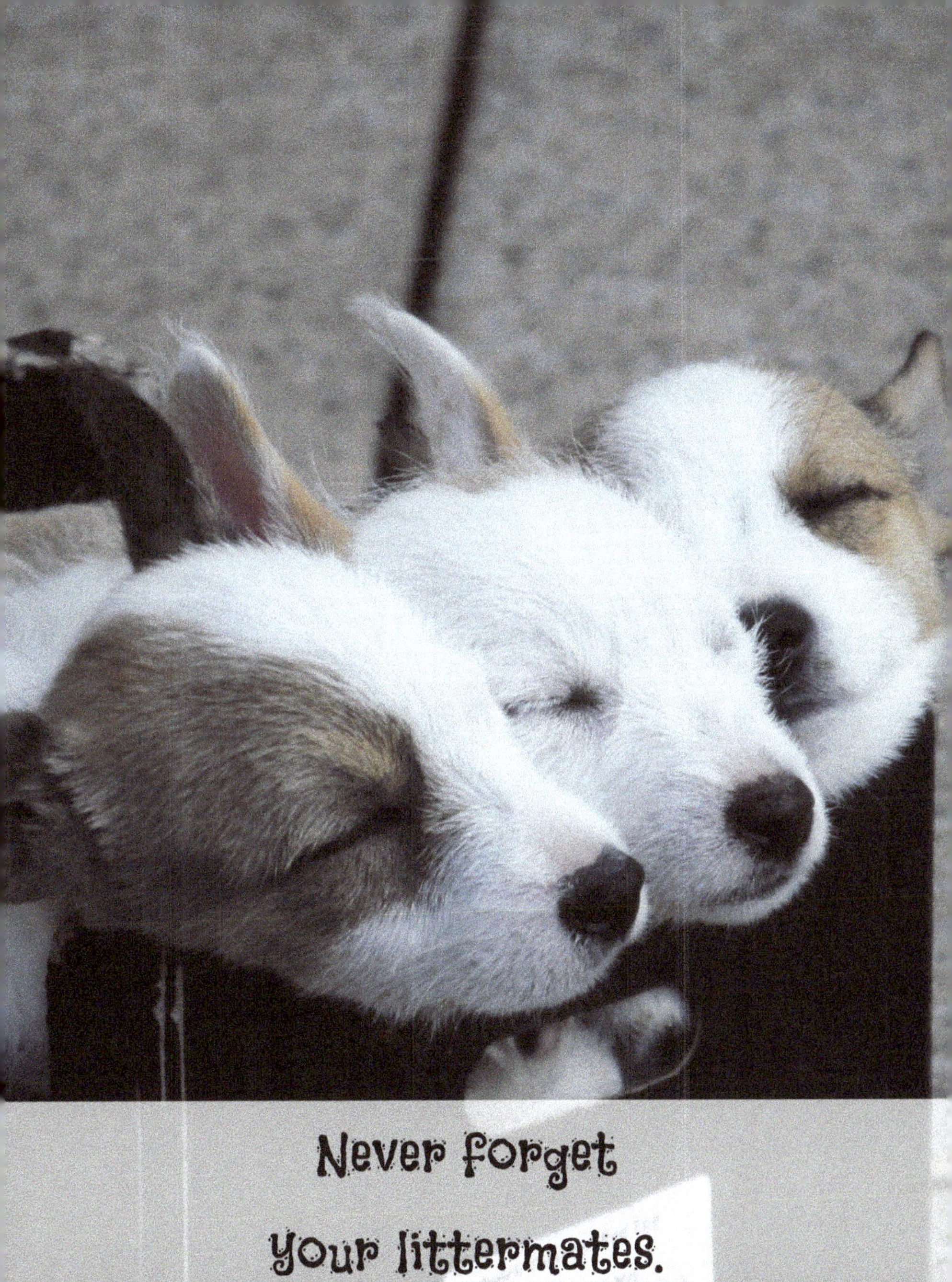

Never forget
your littermates.

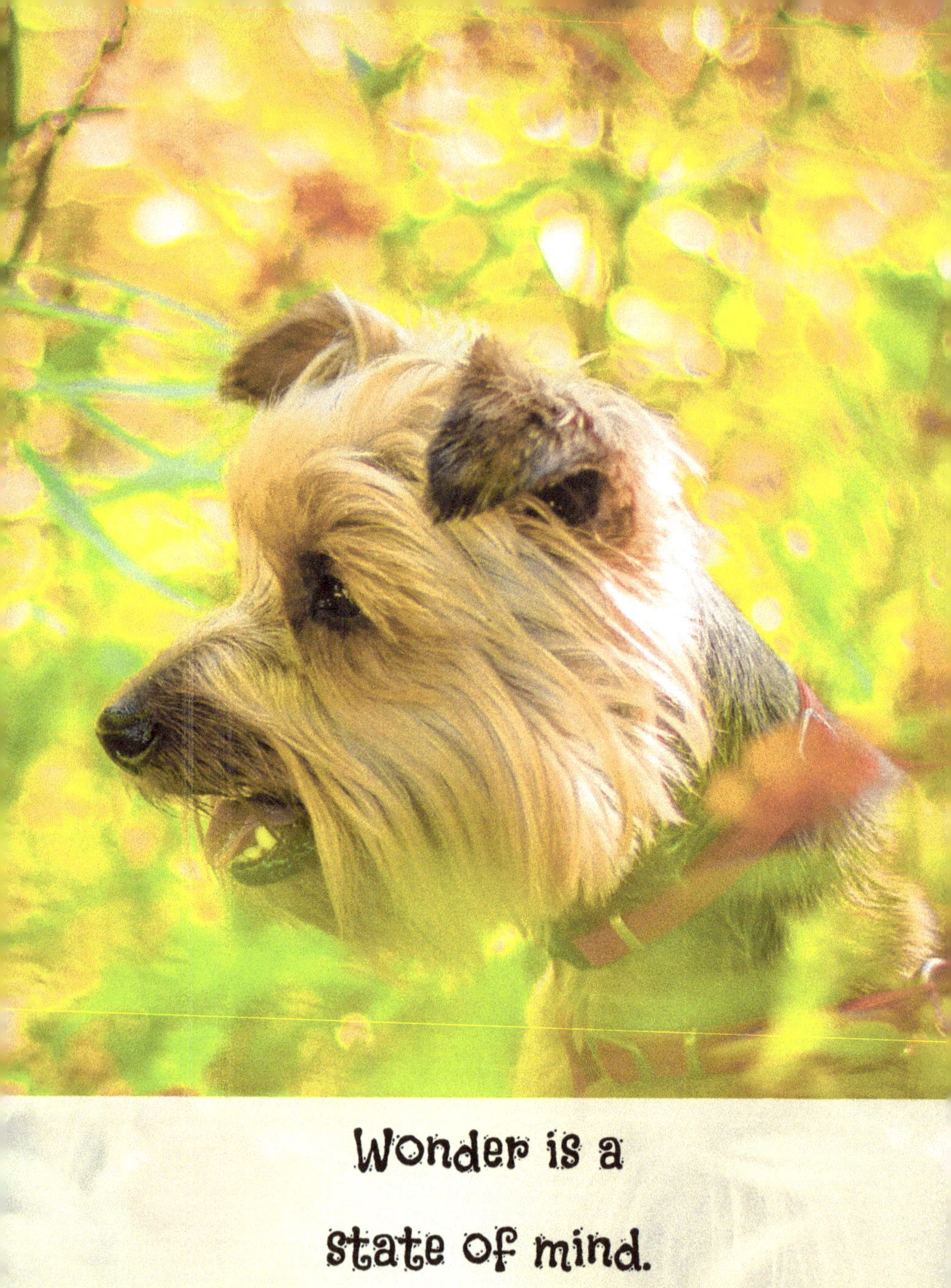

Wonder is a
state of mind.

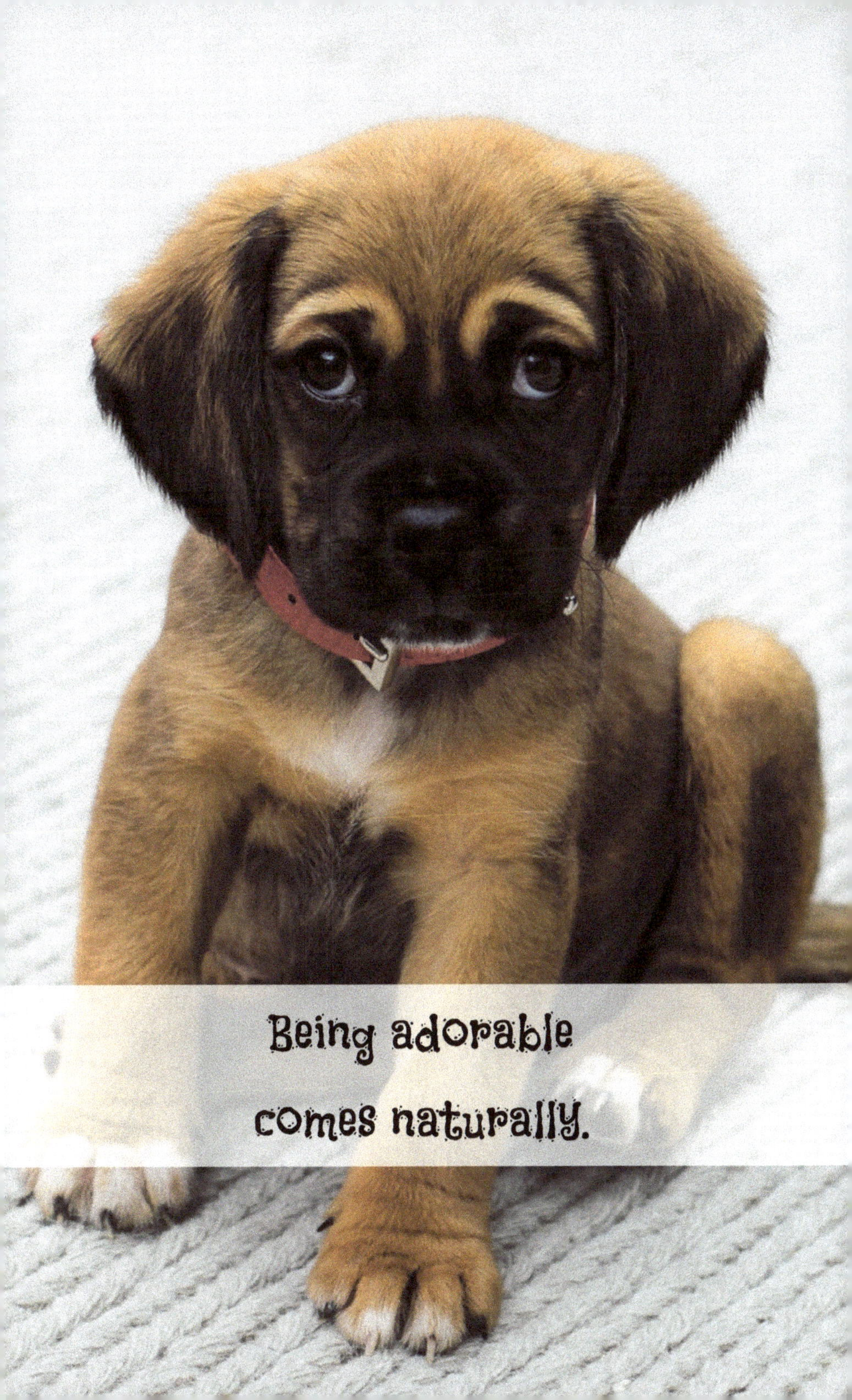

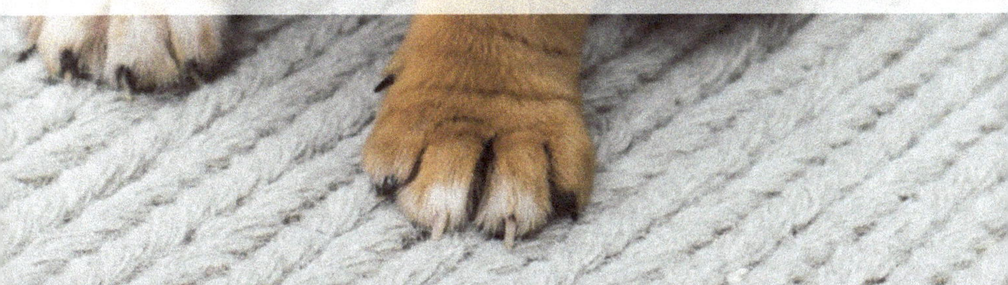
Being adorable
comes naturally.

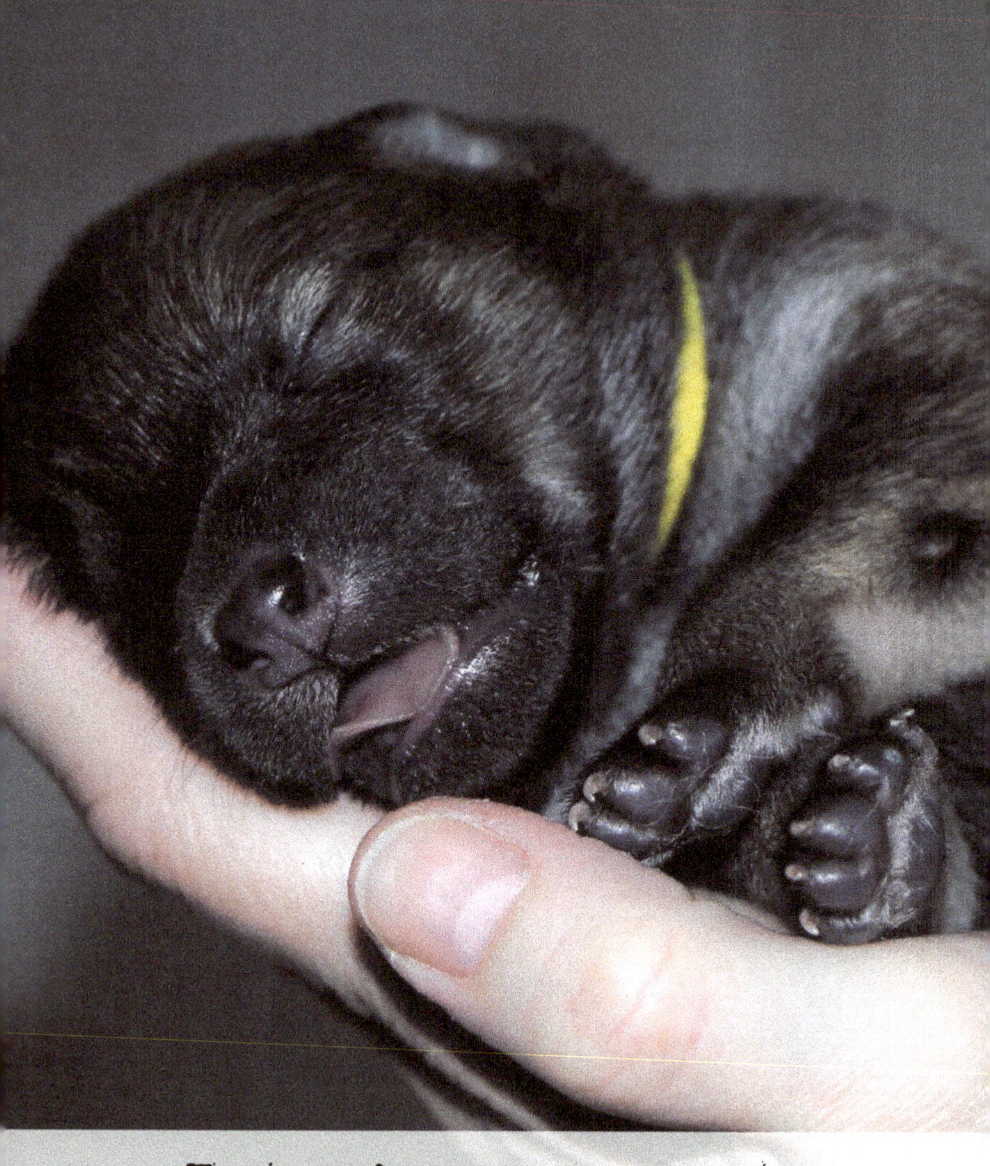

Frequent naps prepare you
for the next expedition.

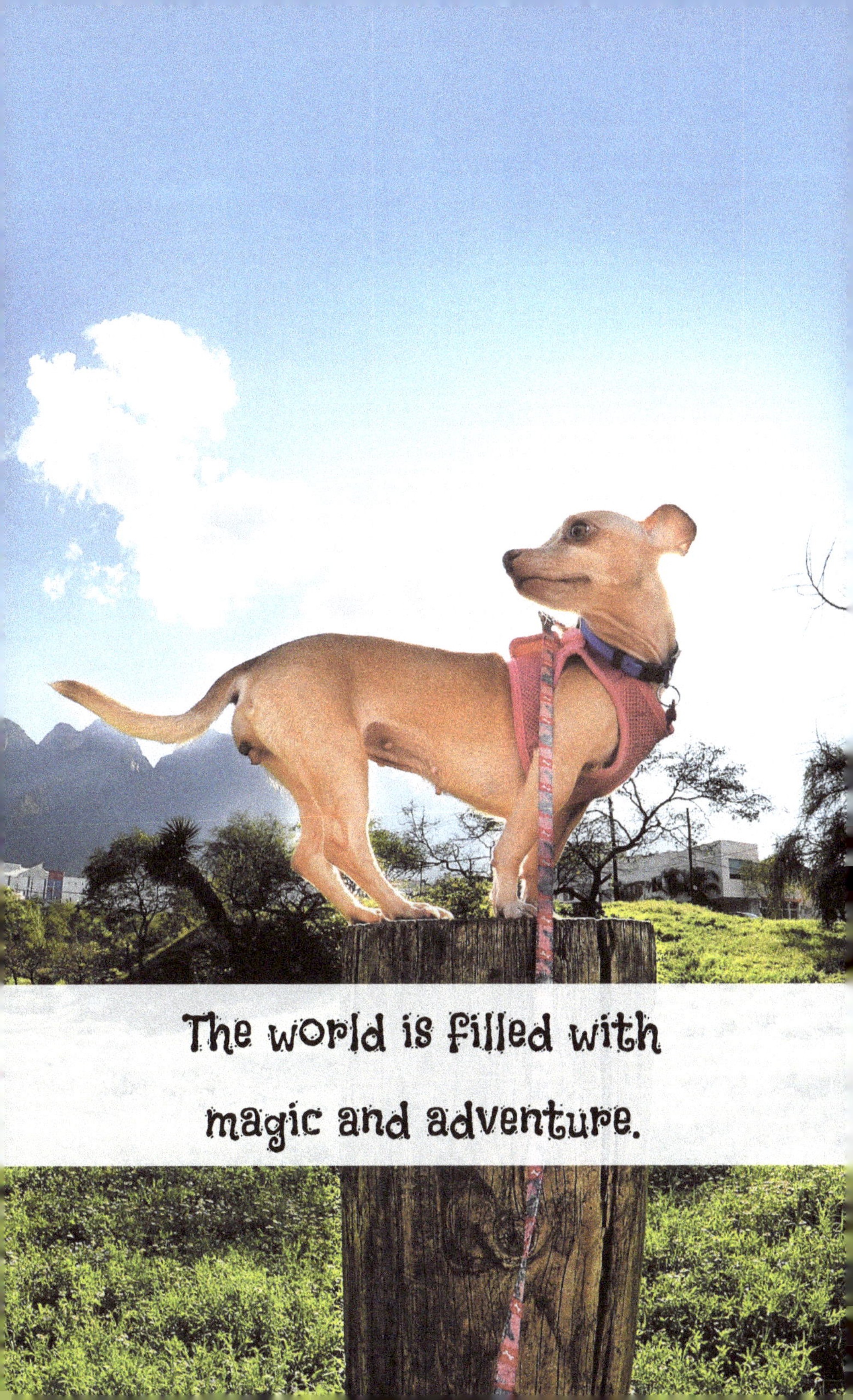

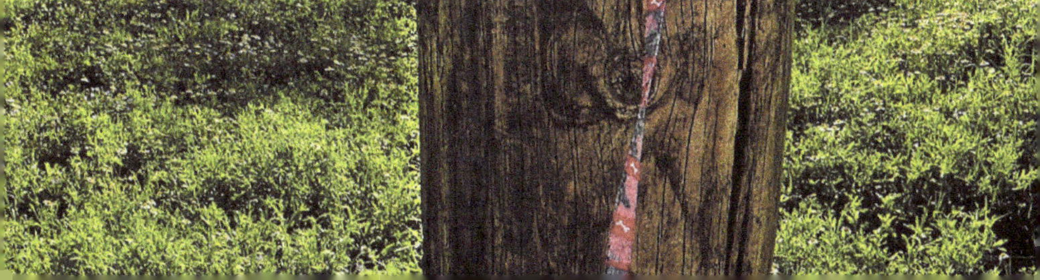

The world is filled with
magic and adventure.

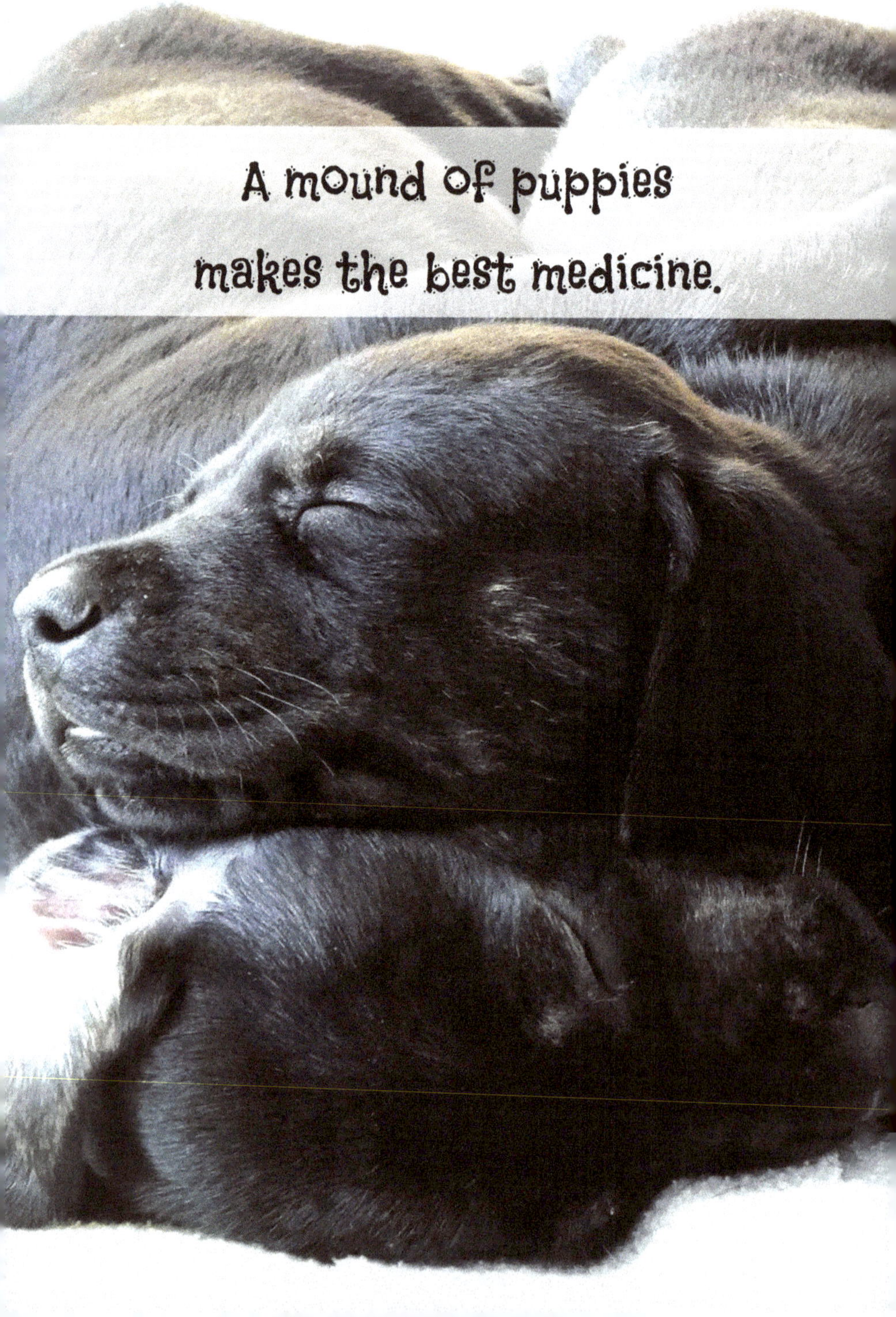

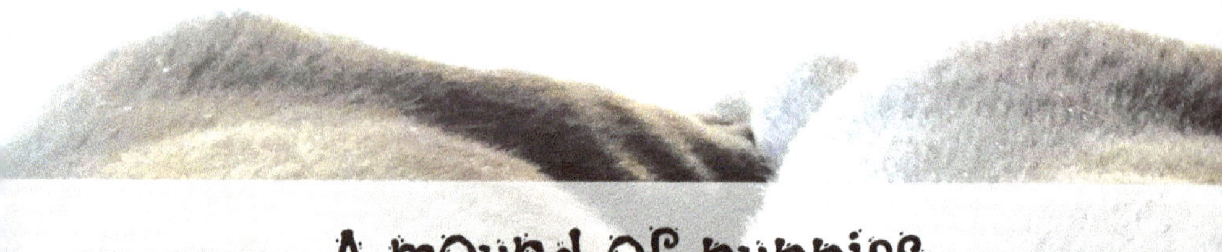

A mound of puppies
makes the best medicine.

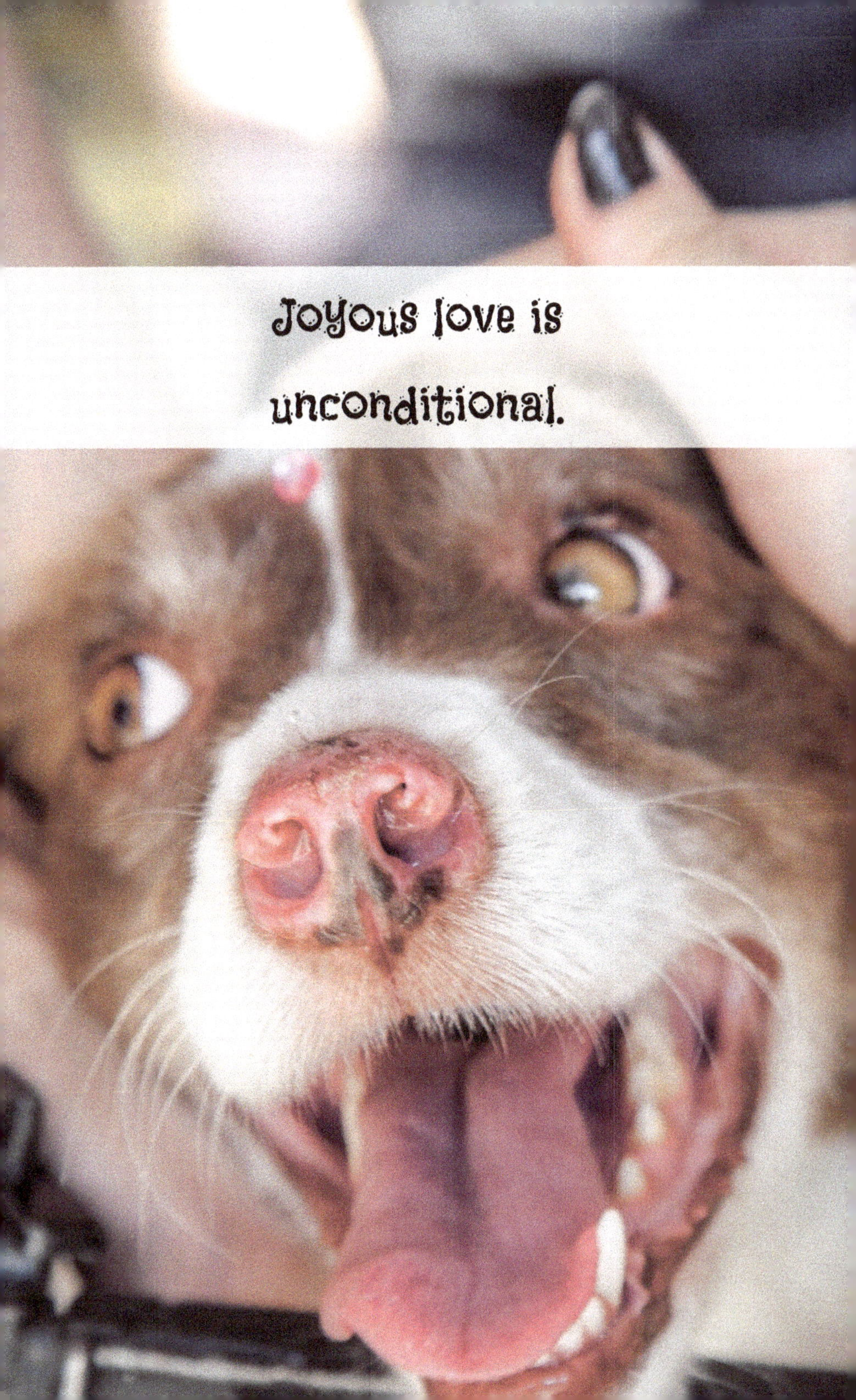

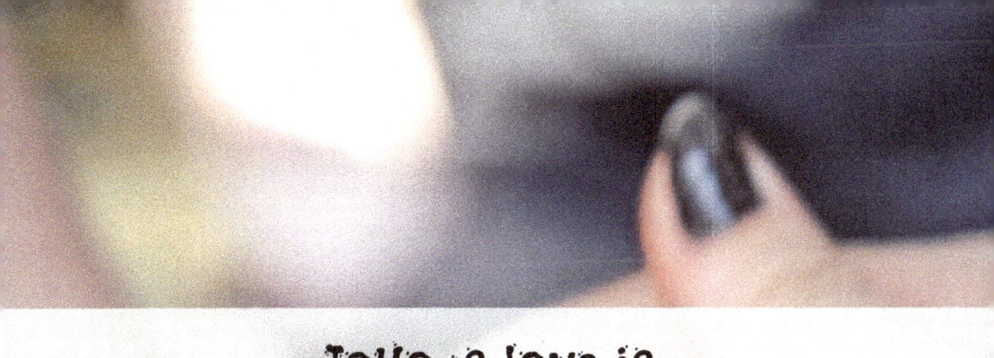
Joyous love is
unconditional.

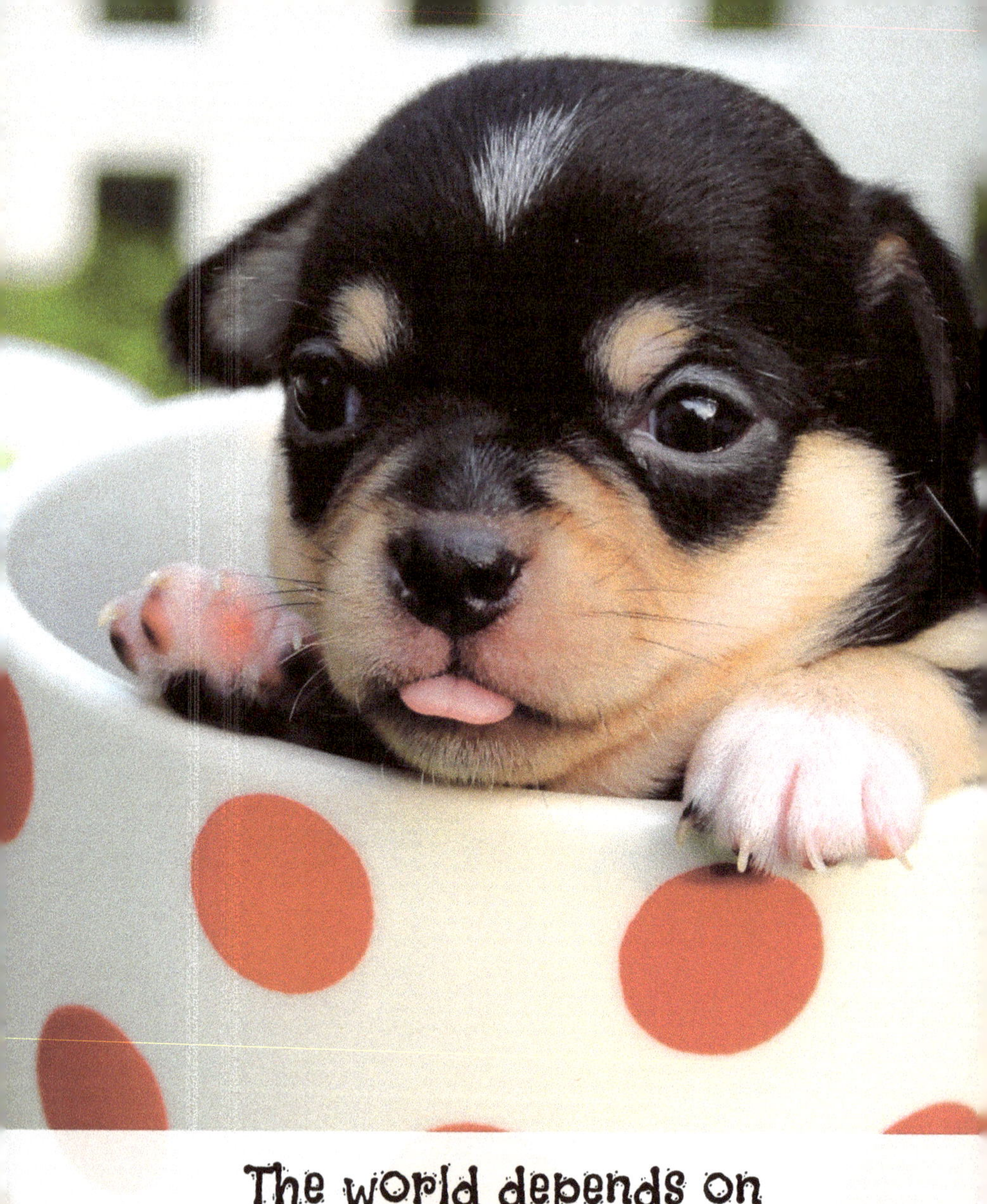

The world depends on
unnecessary cuteness.

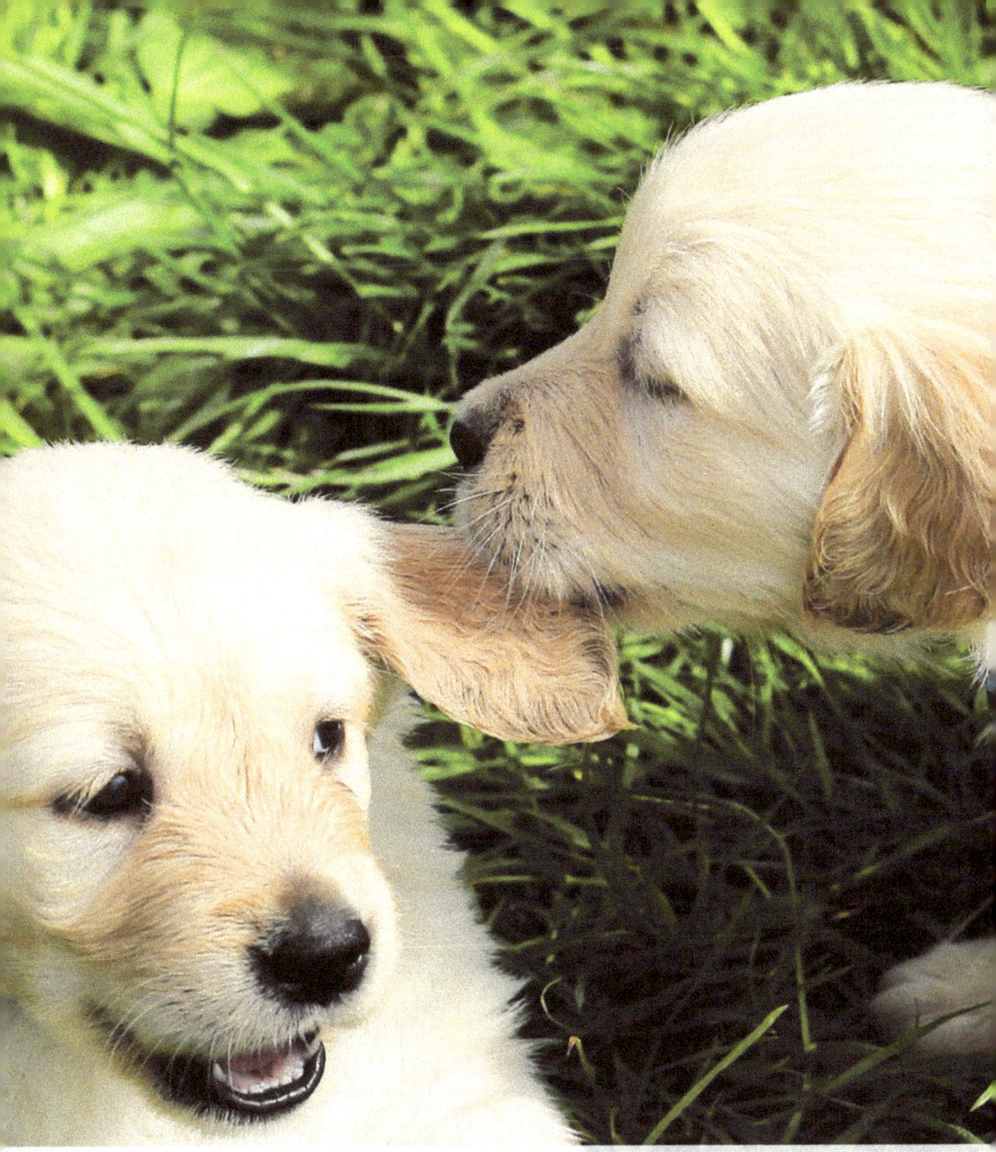

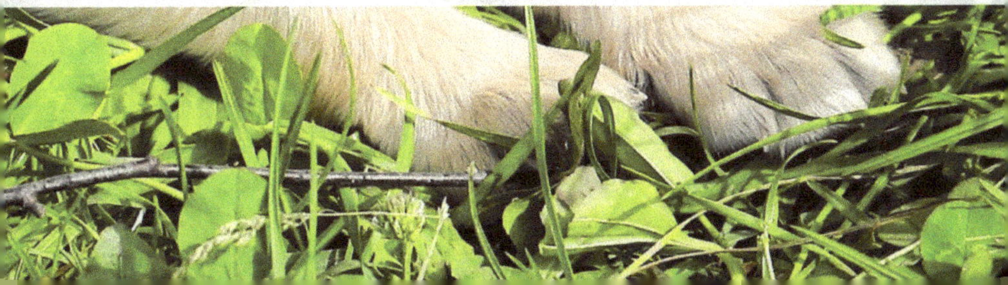
A playful spirit
strengthens the soul.

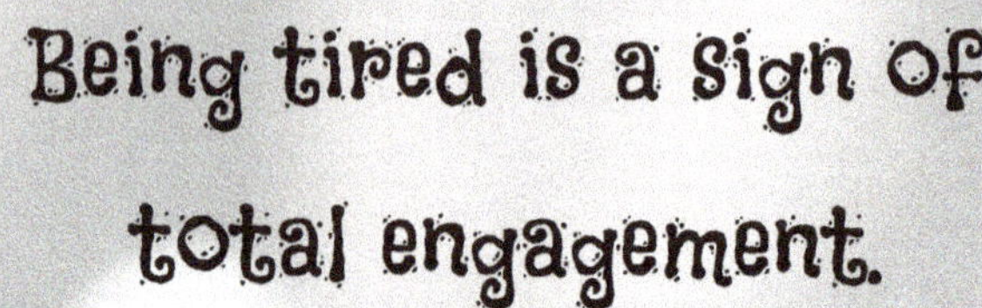
Being tired is a sign of
total engagement.

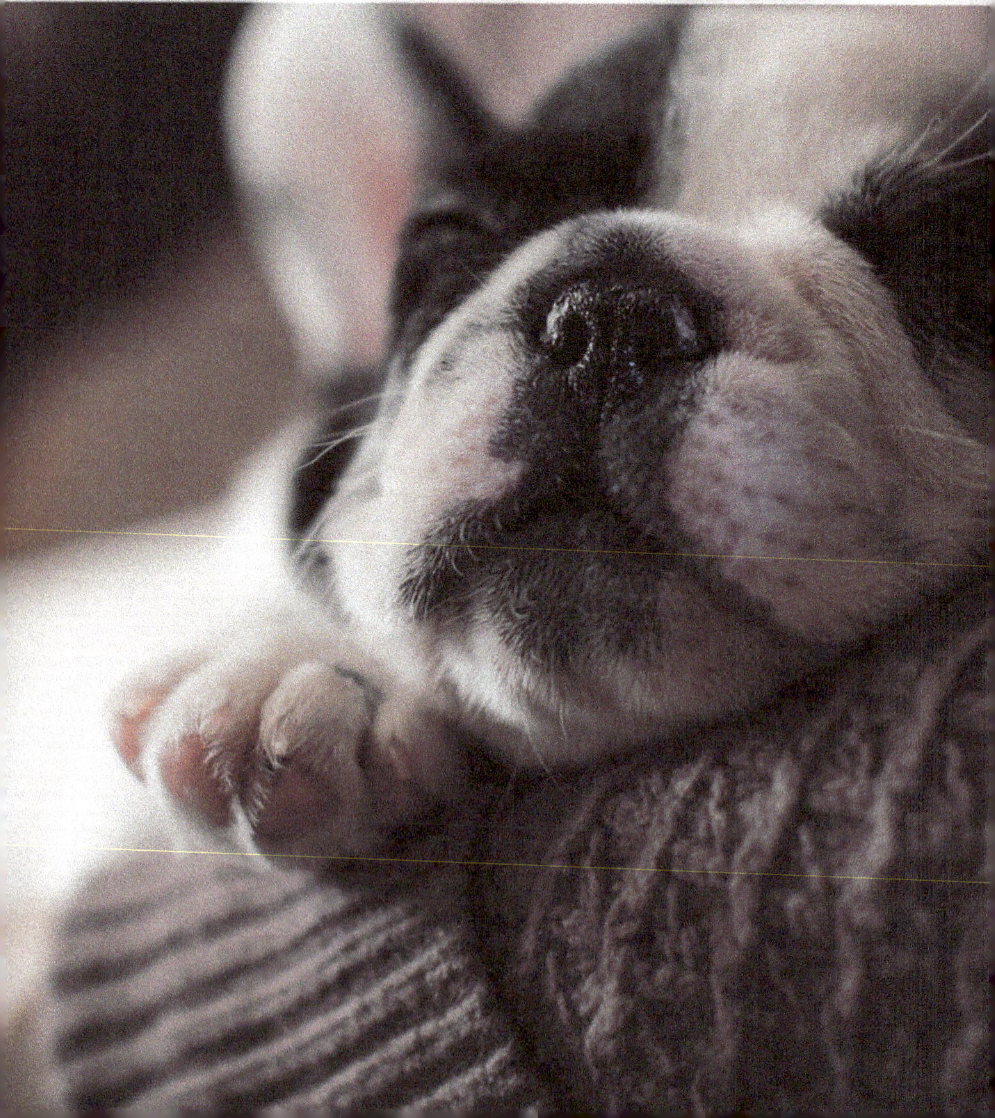

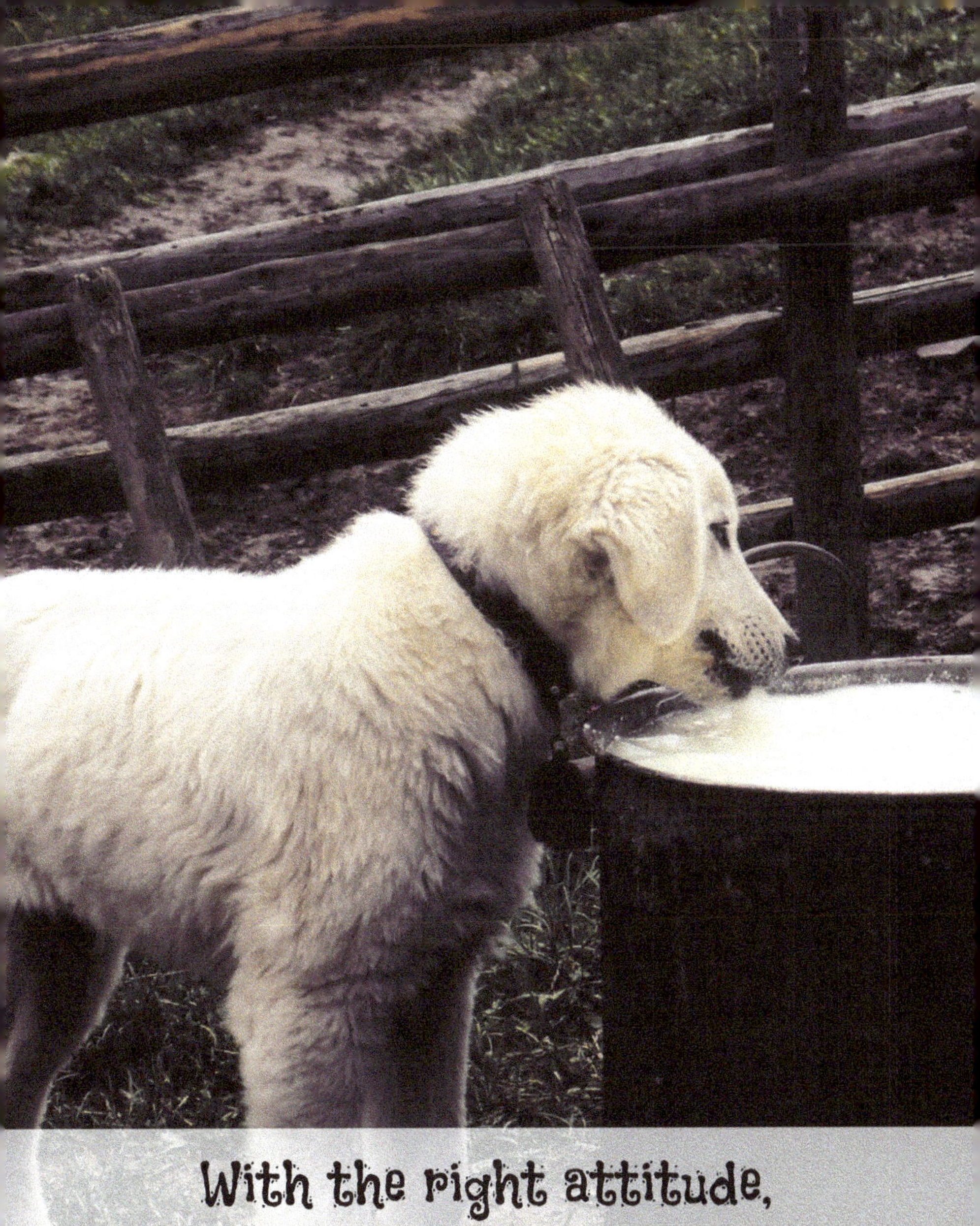

With the right attitude,
nothing is off limits.

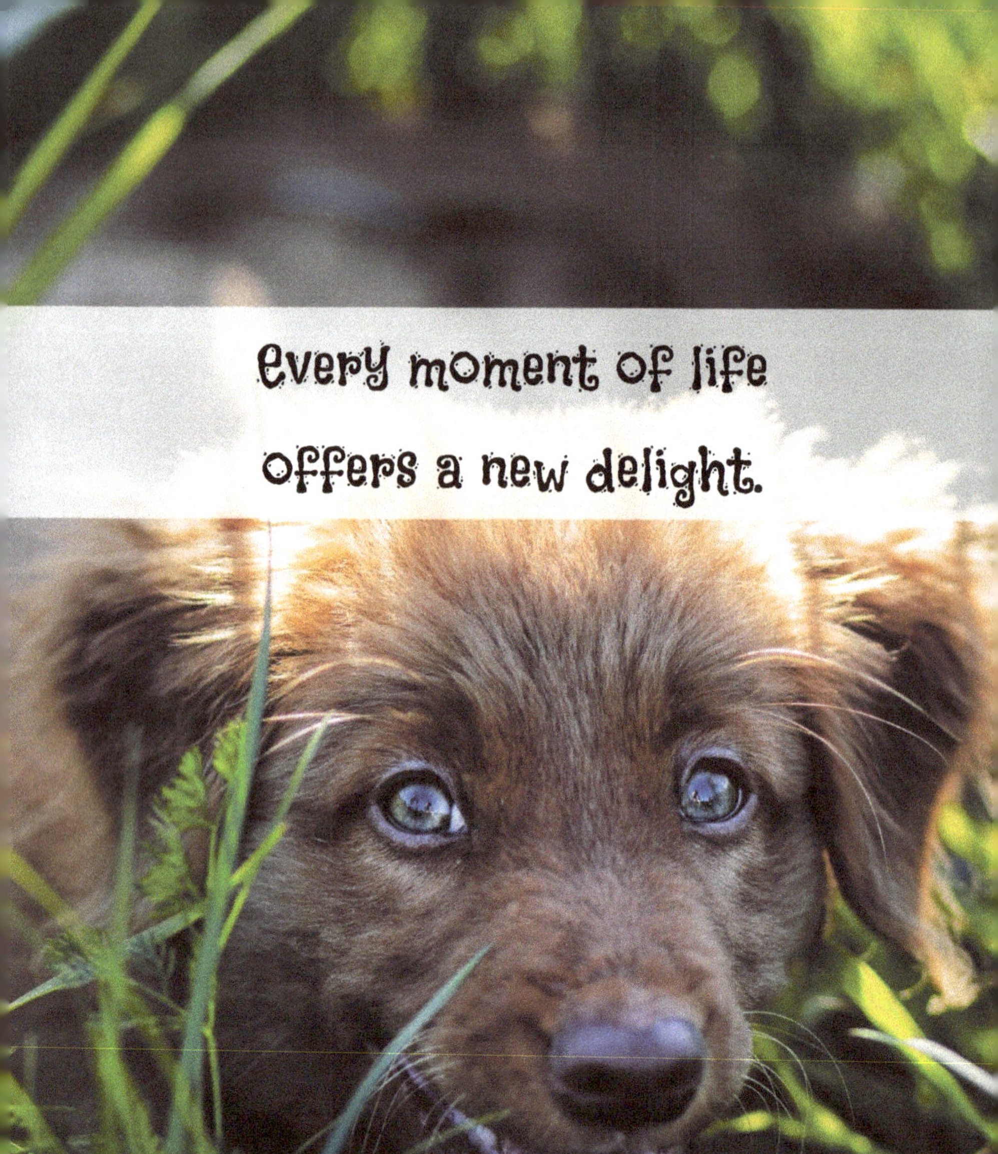

every moment of life
offers a new delight.

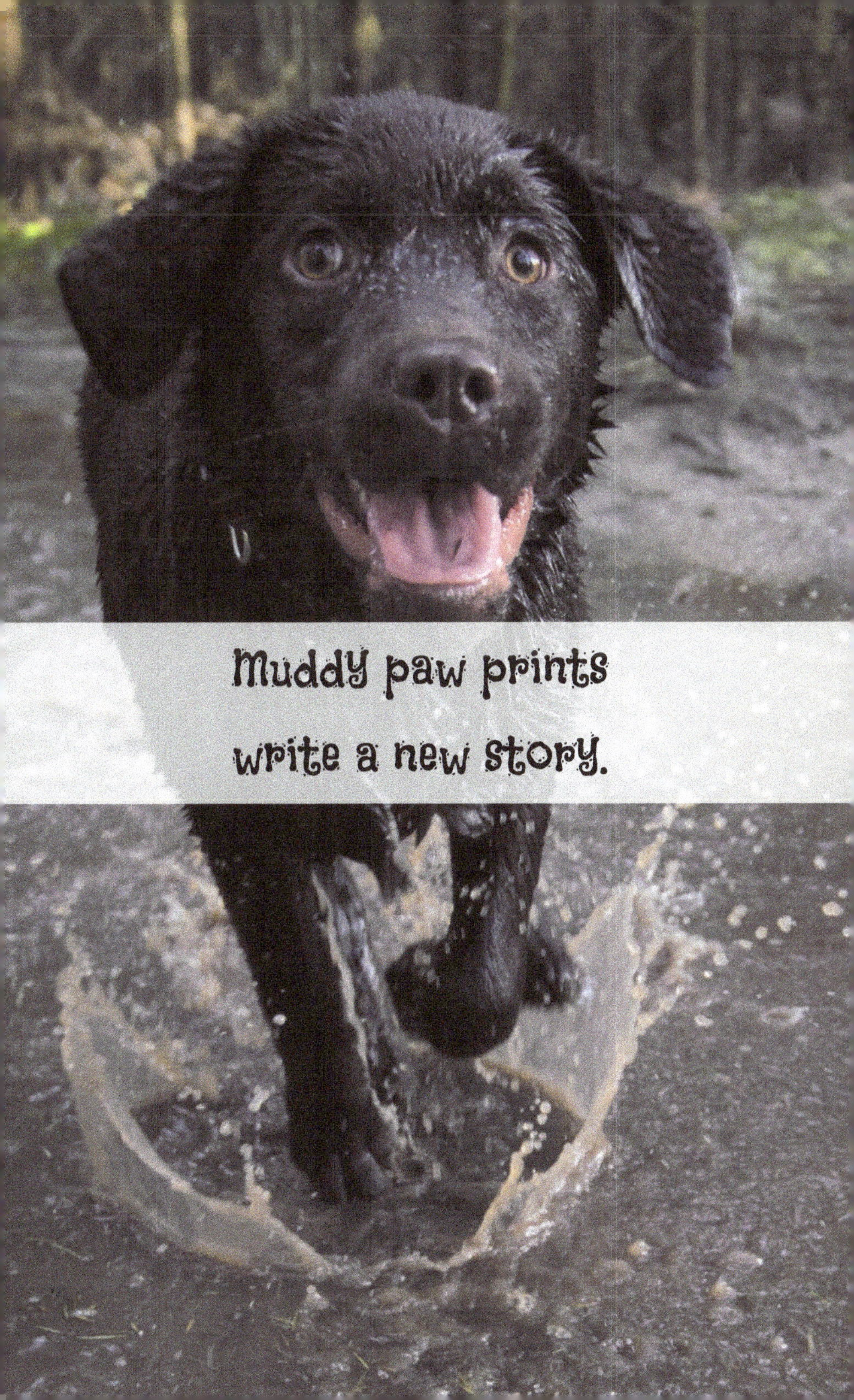

Muddy paw prints
write a new story.

About the Author

Laine Cunningham's books take readers on adventures around the world. *The Family Made of Dust* is set in the Australian Outback, while *Reparation* is a novel of the American Great Plains. Her women's travel adventure memoir *Woman Alone: A Six-Month Journey Through the Australian Outback* appeals to fans of *Wild* and *Eat Pray Love*. Her work has received multiple awards including the Hackney and the James Jones Fellowship, and has been published by *Reed, Birmingham Arts Journal*, and the annual anthology by *Writer's Digest*. She is the senior editor of *Sunspot Literary Journal*.

Fiction

The Family Made of Dust
Beloved
Reparation

Nonfiction

Woman Alone

On the Wallaby Track: Australian Words and Phrases

Seven Sisters: Messages from Aboriginal Australia

Writing While Female or Black or Gay

The Wisdom of Puppies
The Wisdom of Babies
The Wisdom of Weddings

The Zen of Travel
The Zen of Gardening
Zen in the Stable
The Zen of Chocolate
The Zen of Dogs

Bikes of Berlin
Necropolises of New Orleans I & II
Ruins of Rome I & II
Ancients of Assisi I & II
Panoramas of Portugal
Nuances of New York
Glimpses of Germany
Impressions of Italy
Altitudes of the Alps
Knights Through the Ages
Utopia of the Unicorn
Portraits of Paris
Flourishes of France